INDUSTRIAL APPLICATIONS OF MACHINE LEARNING

AF824494

INDUSTRIAL APPLICATIONS OF MACHINE LEARNING

Deepthi Kalavala
Ms. P. Sree Lakshmi
Prof (Dr.) Umakant Dinkar Butkar
Sushama Dhumal-Khanvilkar

NAMYA PRESS.com

Published by

Namya Press

India: 213, Vardan House, 7/28 Ansari Road Darya Ganj - Delhi India 110002
USA: 10685-B Hazelhurst Dr. # 31013 Houston, Texas USA - 77043
Email: namyapress@gmail.com
Website: https://namyapress.com

Edition	:	First Published in 2023 (Namya Press)
Title	:	Industrial Applications of Machine Learning
Authors	:	Deepthi Kalavala, Ms. P. Sree Lakshmi, Prof (Dr.) Umakant Dinkar Butkar, Sushama Dhumal-Khanvilkar
ISBN	:	978-93-5545-221-4
Copyright	:	© Deepthi Kalavala, Ms. P. Sree Lakshmi, Prof (Dr.) Umakant Dinkar Butkar, Sushama Dhumal-Khanvilkar 2023 All Rights Reserved

This book is being sold on the condition that it cannot be used commercially or in any other form without the prior written permission of the publisher. This book cannot be republished or sold or rented. And it cannot be operated among readers in book-binding or any other form. All these conditions will also apply to the buyer of the book. All rights of copyright are reserved in this context.

This book has been published with all efforts taken in making the material error-free after the consent of the author. However, the author and the publisher do not assume and hereby disclaim any liability of any part for loss, damage, or disruption caused by error or omissions.

Dedicated to

Our Family

&

Our Current Working

Organization

Preface

Machine learning is a rapidly burgeoning field with increasing applications to industry. It is transforming the way that businesses make decisions by providing solutions to complex problems in a fraction of the time and effort that traditional methods have required. This book is designed to introduce industrial professionals to the techniques and methods used in machine learning and provide them with a roadmap to effectively apply them in their own fields.

The topics covered in this book range from fundamental supervised and unsupervised learning techniques, to more complex neural networks and deep learning algorithms. We will also discuss topics such as data mining, predictive modeling, and natural language processing (NLP). Finally, practical applications of machine learning in the domains of predictive analytics, computer vision, robotics, and control technology are discussed.

With the abundance of data available across multiple industries, machine learning is becoming a valuable tool for industrial professionals. Through understanding the components of machine learning, exploring its various techniques, and applying its problem-solving capabilities, professionals everywhere will be able to leverage its power to improve decision-making and increase efficiency.

Contents

Preface *vii*
1. Introduction of Machine Learning 1
2. Fraud Detection and Anomaly Detection 20
3. Machine Learning in Healthcare 40
4. Machine Learning in Finance: Revolutionizing the Future of Financial Analysis 63
5. Industrial and Manufacturing Processes Using Machine Learning 82
6. Machine Learning in Robotics and Autonomous Systems 101
7. Machine Learning in Cybersecurity 125
8. Machine Learning Emerging Trends and Future Directions 147

1

Introduction of Machine Learning

1.1. UNDERSTANDING MACHINE LEARNING'S FUNDAMENTALS

Machine learning (ML) is a subfield of artificial intelligence (AI) that focuses on the development of algorithms and techniques that enable computers to learn from data and make predictions or decisions without special programming. In other words, ML algorithms learn patterns and relationships from examples or past experiences and use that knowledge to make informed predictions or decisions based on new, unseen data. The basic principle of machine learning is that computers can learn from data and improve their performance over time by recognizing patterns and making predictions or decisions based on those patterns. ML algorithms are designed to automatically learn and adapt to data without being individually programmed for each specific task. This makes ML particularly useful in complex and data-rich domains where traditional rule-based programming methods may be difficult or impractical to apply. To better understand machine learning, let's delve into its basic components, types, and learning. Parts of Machine Learning:

Data: Data is the foundation of machine learning. It consists of examples or cases that the ML algorithm uses to learn patterns and make predictions or decisions. Data can take different forms, such as structured data (e.g. databases, spreadsheets) or unstructured data (e.g. text documents, images, videos).

Features: Features are individual measurable properties or characteristics of the data that the ML algorithm uses to make predictions or decisions. Features are selected or extracted from the raw data and serve as inputs to the ML model. Feature quality and relevance play a crucial role in the performance of an ML algorithm.

ML Model: An ML model is a mathematical or computer representation of the relationships and patterns learned from data. A model captures a description between input properties and output predictions or decisions. It is a core component of an ML system and is responsible for making predictions or decisions based on new, unseen information.

Training: Training feeds the ML model with labelled data to learn patterns and relationships. Tagged data consists of input properties and their corresponding actual output values or target identifiers. During training, the ML algorithm adjusts the internal parameters of the model to minimize the difference between the predicted outputs and the actual outputs.

Evaluation: Evaluation evaluates the performance of the trained ML model with new, unseen data. Model predictions or decisions are compared with actual values or records in the assessment data. Evaluation metrics such as precision, accuracy, recall, or root mean square error are used to measure the performance of an ML model.

Types of Machine Learning

Machine learning can be divided into three main types based on the learning process and the availability of labelled data:

- **Supervised learning:** Supervised learning algorithms learn from labelled data, where each instance of the training data has a corresponding target entity or result value. The goal is to learn how to map input functions to output identifiers so that you can make predictions or make decisions based on new, unseen data. Common supervised learning tasks include classification and regression.
- **Unsupervised learning:** Unsupervised learning algorithms learn from unlabelled data where only input features are provided without target labels or output values. The goal of unsupervised learning is to find inherent patterns, structures, or relationships in data. Clustering and dimensionality reduction are typical tasks in unsupervised learning.
- **Reinforcement learning:** Reinforcement learning means that the agent learns to interact with the environment and make decisions to maximize the cumulative reward. The agent learns through trial and error and receives feedback on its actions in the form of rewards or punishments. The goal is to learn the optimal policy or strategy to achieve long-term benefits. Reinforcement learning is often applied to sequential decision tasks.

MACHINE LEARNING PROCESS

The machine learning process consists of several interrelated steps that turn data into a trained ML model capable of making predictions or decisions. Typical steps in the ML process are:

- **Data preprocessing:** In this step, the raw data is prepared and converted into a suitable format for the ML algorithm. This includes tasks such as cleaning data by handling missing values, handling outliers, and normalizing or scaling data to ensure consistency.
- **Feature Selection/Extraction:** Feature selection or extraction is the process of identifying the most important and informative features from the data. Its purpose is to reduce the dimensionality of the data and remove pale or unnecessary features that can hinder learning. Feature extraction techniques such as principal component analysis (PCA) or word embedding can be used to transform the data into a lower dimensional representation.
- **Model selection:** Model selection involves the appropriate ML algorithm or model that best fits the given problem. The choice of model depends on the type of task (classification, regression, clustering, etc.), the nature of the data and the available resources.
- **Training:** In the training phase, the selected ML model is trained using labelled data. A model is presented with its input properties and their corresponding target identifiers or output values. The model iteratively adjusts its internal parameters using optimization algorithms to minimize the difference between predicted outputs and actual outputs.
- **Evaluation:** After training, the performance of the ML model is evaluated using evaluation data that the model did not see during training. Evaluation metrics are used to measure model accuracy, precision, recall, or other performance metrics. This step helps assess the generalizability of the model and its ability to make accurate predictions or decisions based on new, unseen data.
- **Model optimization and hyperparameter tuning:** Model optimization involves fine-tuning the ML algorithm to improve its performance. The hyperparameters that determine the behaviour and complexity of the ML model are tuned for optimal performance. Techniques such as grid search, random search or Bayesian optimization can be used to explore different combinations of hyperparameters and find the best settings for the model.

- **Prediction/Decision Making:** Once an ML model is trained and optimized, it can be used to make predictions or decisions based on new, unseen data. The model takes inputs as input and produces corresponding predictions or decisions as output. Predictions or decisions can be further analysed or used to take appropriate actions in real applications.

Challenges and future directions in machine learning

Although machine learning has made significant progress, researchers and practitioners are actively considering a number of challenges and future trends.

- **Data quality and quantity:** Availability of high-quality, labelled data is critical to training accurate ML models. Collecting, cleaning, and labelling large data sets can be time-consuming and expensive. Techniques for handling limited labelled data, knowledge augmentation and generative models are being developed to address this challenge.
- **Interpretability and explain ability:** As ML models become more complex, interpreting and explaining their decisions or predictions becomes difficult. The goal of interpretive ML research is to develop techniques that provide transparency and explanations for ML algorithms so that users understand and trust model outputs.
- **Ethical and justice considerations:** ML algorithms can inadvertently reinforce biases and discriminate against certain groups if not carefully developed and used. Ensuring fairness, accountability and transparency in ML algorithms is an ongoing challenge. Methods to identify and mitigate bias, as well as guidelines and regulations, are being developed to address the ethical implications.
- **Deep Learning and Beyond:** Deep Learning, a subfield of ML based on neural networks, has shown significant success in several areas. Future directions include addressing challenges in training deep learning models for limited labelled data, reducing computational requirements and improving interpretability. Alternative learning paradigms such as reinforcement learning and unsupervised learning are also being explored for more efficient and effective learning algorithms.

Machine learning is a powerful approach to data analysis and decision making that allows computers to learn from data and make predictions or decisions without special programming. It includes a variety of algorithms, techniques and processes that make it possible to extract valuable insights from data. By understanding the components of ML, the different types of learning and the ML process, we can understand the basics of this exciting field.

Machine learning continues to advance rapidly, and ongoing research focuses on challenges related to data quality, interpretability, fairness, and ethical considerations. The exciting development of deep learning and alternative learning paradigms is shaping the future of machine learning, making it a dynamic and promising field for innovation and applications in various fields.

1.2. DIFFERENT MACHINE LEARNING TECHNIQUES

Machine learning (ML) can be classified into three main types based on the learning process and the availability of labelled data supervised learning, unsupervised learning, and reinforcement learning. Each type has its own characteristics, algorithms and applications. Let's examine these types in more detail:

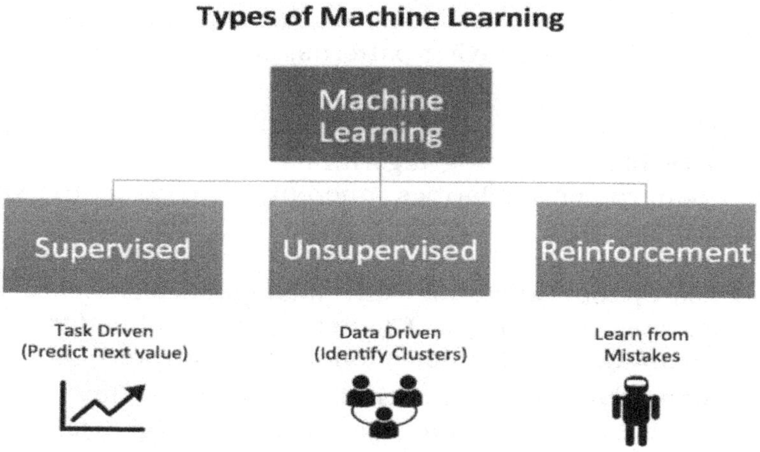

1. Supervised learning: Supervised learning is the most common and widely used type of machine learning. In supervised learning, the ML algorithm learns from labelled data, where each instance of the training dataset has a corresponding target label or output value. The goal is to learn the mapping between input features and output titles, allowing the algorithm to make predictions or make decisions based on new, unseen information.

Supervised learning tasks can be divided into two subtypes:

- **Classification:** In classification tasks, the ML algorithm learns to classify input data into predefined classes or classes. For example, based on features representing email attributes, a classification algorithm can be trained to predict whether we have spam or not. Common classification algorithms include logistic regression, support vector machines (SVM), decision trees, and random forests.

- **Regression:** In regression tasks, the ML algorithm learns to predict continuous numerical values or quantities. Regression is used when the output variable is a continuous value, such as predicting housing prices based on characteristics such as floor space, number of rooms, etc. Linear r e gression, polynomial regression, and neural networks are commonly used algorithms for regression tasks.

Supervised learning requires labelled data for training, and the quality and quantity of labelled data greatly affect the performance of the ML model. The trained model can then generalize the learned patterns and make predictions based on new, unseen data.

2. Unsupervised learning: Unsupervised learning refers to learning from unlabelled data where only input features are provided without target identifiers or output values. In this type of learning, the ML algorithm examines underlying patterns, structures, or relationships in the data.

Unsupervised learning tasks can be divided into two subtypes:

- **Clustering:** Clustering algorithms group similar cases based on patterns or similarities inherent in the data. The goal is to identify natural clusters or subgroups in the dataset. K-means clustering, hierarchical clustering, and DBSCAN (Density-Based Spatial Clustering with Noisy Applications) are common clustering algorithms. Clustering is useful for customer segmentation, outlier detection, and pattern recognition.
- **Dimensionality reduction:** Dimensionality reduction techniques aim to reduce the number of input features while preserving important information. It helps visualize high-dimensional data and extract the most important features. Principal component analysis (PCA) and t-SNE (t-Distributed Stochastic Neighbour Embedding) are popular dimensionality reduction algorithms.

Unsupervised learning is valuable when there is no identified data or when the goal is to find unknown patterns or insights in the data.

3. Reinforcement learning: Reinforcement learning (RL) is a subfield of machine learning that focuses on training agents to make sequential decisions in an environment to maximize cumulative reward.

It is inspired by how humans and animals learn through trial and error while interacting with the world. RL algorithms allow an agent to learn optimal strategies through exploration and exploitation without explicit inspection or labeled datasets.

Main parts of reinforcement learning:

- **Agent:** Learner or decision maker who interacts with the environment. It monitors the current situation, takes action and receives feedback in the form of rewards.
- **Environment:** The external system with which the agent interacts. It gives the agent states, accepts actions, and provides rewards or punishments based on the actions of the agent.
- **State:** Representation of the environment at a given moment. It collects important information that the agent needs to make decisions.
- **Action:** The options available to the agent in each mode. An agent chooses actions based on its policy, which maps states to actions. 5. Reward: a feedback signal indicating the desirability of an agent's action. The agent's goal is to maximize cumulative benefits over time.
- **Practice:** Strategy or behavior of an agent that maps states into actions. It guides the agent's decision-making process.
- **Value function:** the value of a state or state-action pair that represents the expected cumulative reward that an agent can obtain from that state or state-action pair. It directs the agent to evaluate the desirability of various actions or states.

Algorithms of Amplification

- **Q-Learning:** Q-Learning is a model-free RL algorithm that learns an action value function (Q-function). It iteratively updates Q values based on observed benefits and estimated future benefits. The agent uses the Q values to determine the best course of action in a given state.
- **Practicing gradient methods:** These algorithms optimize practice by directly estimating gradients using a sample. They learn by repeatedly adjusting practice to increase the likelihood that performing actions will lead to higher rewards. Practical gradient methods include REINFORCE, Proximal Policy Optimization (PPO), and Trust Region Policy Optimization (TRPO).
- **Deep Q-Network (DQN):** DQN combines Q-learning with deep neural networks to deal with high-dimensional spatial

spaces. It uses a deep neural network known as a Q network to approximate the Q values. DQN introduces repetition of experiences and target networks to stabilize and improve the learning.

- **Actor-critical methods:** Actor-critical algorithms maintain both a policy (actor) and a value function (critic). The actor proposes policy-based actions, the critic evaluates the action using a value function. That approach allows the agent to learn from both political effectiveness and the evaluations of critics.

Applications of Reinforcement Learning

Reinforcement learning has found applications in several areas, including:

- **Gaming:** RL algorithms have achieved significant success in playing games such as chess, Go and video games, surpassing human performance.
- **Robotics:** RL is used to train robots to perform complex tasks such as grasping objects, navigating dynamic environments or mastering locomotive skills.
- **Autonomous vehicles:** RL trains self-driving cars to make decisions based on the environment and traffic conditions.
- **Recommender systems:** RL algorithms can be used to adapt recommendations to users by learning their preferences and optimizing long-term rewards.
- **Healthcare:** RL is used to optimize treatment strategies, drug dosing and resource allocation in healthcare settings. Reinforcement learning provides agents with an efficient framework for making optimal decisions in sequential decision problems. This allows for independent learning, adaptability, and the ability to handle complex tasks without direct supervision.

Hybrid Methods and Other Variations

In addition to the three main types mentioned above, there are hybrid approaches and varieties of machine learning that combine different types of elements:

1. **Semi-supervised learning:** Semi-supervised learning combines labelled and unlabelled information for training. It uses both a small amount of labelled data and a larger amount of unlabelled data to improve learning. Semi-supervised learning is useful when labelling large datasets is expensive or time-consuming.

2. **Transfer learning:** Transfer learning uses knowledge learned in one task or domain to improve learning in another related task or domain. The pretrained knowledge of the source task is transferred and refined by the limited labelled information of the target task. Transfer learning reduces the need for extensive training for the target task and enables faster learning.
3. **Online Learning:** Also known as incremental learning or lifelong learning, online learning involves learning from a continuous stream of incoming data. The ML model is constantly updated as new information emerges, allowing the model to adapt and learn in real time. Online learning is useful when the distribution of information changes over time or when new cases need to be handled incrementally.
4. **Deep Learning:** Deep learning is a subfield of ML that focuses on using multilayer neural networks to learn hierarchical representations of data. Deep learning has made significant progress in various fields such as image recognition, natural language processing, and speech synthesis. Deep learning models such as Convolutional Neural Networks (CNNs) and Recurrent Neural Networks (RNNs) learn complex patterns and relationships in data, enabling powerful predictions and decisions.

Machine learning includes different types, each with its own characteristics, algorithms and applications. Supervised learning, unsupervised learning and reinforcement learning are the main types of ML. Supervised learning learns from labelled data to make predictions or make decisions, while unsupervised learning examines patterns in unlabelled data. Reinforcement learning focuses on learning by interacting with the environment to maximize rewards. Hybrid methods and variants such as semi-supervised learning, transfer learning, online learning and deep learning expand the capabilities and applications of machine learning. With this kind of understanding, researchers and practitioners can choose the most appropriate approach to solve specific problems and unlock the potential of machine learning in various fields.

1.3. REINFORCEMENT, SUPERVISED AND UNSUPERVISED LEARNING

Reinforcement learning (RL) is a type of machine learning in which an agent learns how to interact with the environment to maximize cumulative reward. An agent works in an environment and based on received feedback or reward, it learns to act optimally to achieve long-term goals. The learning process of reinforcement learning can be visualized using the following diagram:

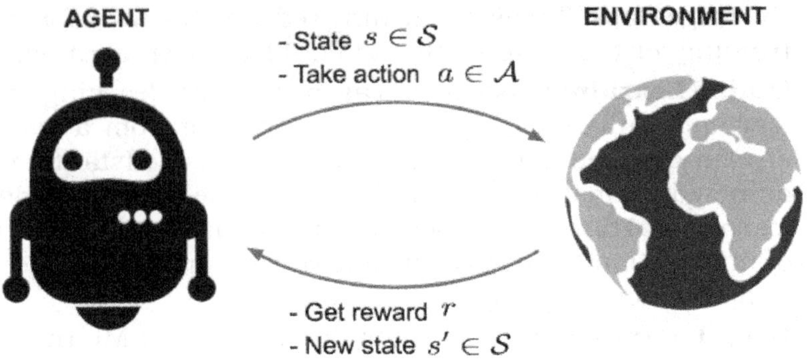

Reinforcement Learning

In RL, an agent interacts with the environment by monitoring its current state, choosing an action to perform, and receiving feedback in the form of rewards or punishments. The goal of the agent is to learn a policy that represents a mapping of states and actions that maximize the cumulative reward over time. Politics can be deterministic or stochastic depending on whether it chooses actions deterministically or probabilistically. Reinforcement learning is typically used for sequential decision-making tasks where an agent must learn how to behave in an environment to achieve a certain goal. Examples include training an autonomous vehicle to navigate traffic, teaching a robot to perform complex tasks, or developing strategies to play games such as chess or go.

Supervised Learning

Supervised learning refers to a guided approach where learners receive structured guidance and support throughout the learning process. This involves providing learners with precise instructions, scaffolding and feedback so that they can effectively acquire new knowledge and skills. This approach is often used in educational settings, training programs, and online courses to improve learning outcomes.

In Supervised learning, the teacher or tutor takes an active role in guiding students through the material. They provide clear instructions, break complex concepts into smaller, more manageable chunks, and provide support when students encounter difficulties. The goal is to gradually transfer responsibility from the teacher to the student, encouraging independent learning over time.

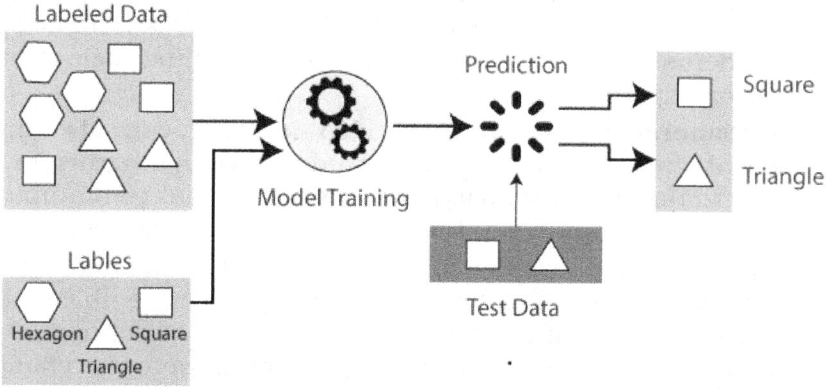

Supervised learning

Supervised learning can take different forms depending on the context and learning objectives. Here are some of the more common strategies and techniques used in supervised learning:

- **Direct instruction:** The teacher presents information or clearly demonstrates his skills and gives step-by-step instructions and examples. Learners observe and imitate the actions of the teacher and gradually develop their understanding and competence.
- **Scaffolding:** The teacher provides temporary support to help students bridge the gap between current knowledge and desired learning outcomes. This support may include prompts, suggestions, models, graphic organizers, or partial solutions that gradually disappear as students acquire skills.
- **Modelling:** The teacher models the desired behaviour or thought process and shows the students how to approach the task or problem. Learners observe the activity and then try to imitate or reproduce it.
- **Think aloud:** The teacher talks about his thought process when solving a problem or completing a task. This technique helps learners understand cognitive stages and promotes metacognitive skills.
- **Guided Exercise:** Students participate in structured exercises under the guidance and supervision of a teacher. The teacher

gives feedback, corrects misunderstandings and gives suggestions for improvement.

- **Formative assessment:** The instructor assesses students' progress during the learning process and provides feedback on their strengths and areas of development. This feedback helps students identify their learning gaps and adjust their strategies accordingly.
- **Collaborative Learning:** Guided learning can also include collaborative activities where students work together in pairs or groups. This approach encourages mutual communication, discussion and the sharing of ideas and perspectives.

Benefits of guided learning include increased student engagement, better understanding of complex concepts, better problem-solving skills and improved self-confidence. By providing structured support and guidance, guided learning can help learners overcome challenges and achieve deeper learning outcomes. It is worth noting that guided learning is not intended to replace other teaching methods such as inquiry-based learning or independent study. Instead, it can be used in conjunction with these approaches to create a balanced and effective learning experience that meets the needs of diverse learners.

Unsupervised Learning

Unsupervised learning is a type of machine learning where a model learns patterns and structures in data without special supervision or labelled examples. Unlike supervised learning, which relies on labelled data to make predictions or classifications, unsupervised learning algorithms operate on unlabelled data and attempt to find patterns, relationships, and structures inherent in the dataset.

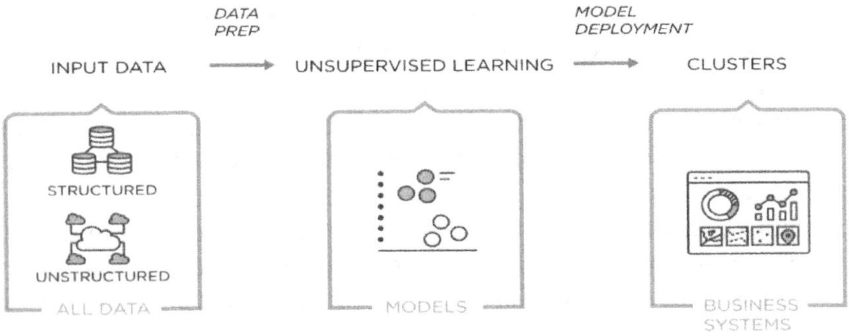

Unsupervised learning

The goal of unsupervised learning is to explore and extract valuable insights, uncover hidden patterns, and better understand the underlying structure of data. It is often used for tasks such as clustering, dimensionality reduction, and outlier detection.

Here are some of the more common techniques used in unsupervised learning:

- **Clustering:** Clustering algorithms group similar data points based on their characteristics. The goal is to identify clusters or groups of data points that are similar to each other and different from data points in other clusters. K-means, hierarchical clustering, and DBSCAN are popular clustering algorithms.
- **Dimensionality reduction:** Dimensionality reduction techniques aim to reduce the number of features or variables in a dataset while preserving important information. This helps visualize high-dimensional data and remove noise or irrelevant features. Principal component analysis (PCA) and t-SNE (t-Distributed Stochastic Neighbor Embedding) are commonly used dimensionality reduction techniques.
- **Anomaly detection:** Anomaly detection identifies rare or unusual data points or patterns that do not conform to the standard. This technique is useful for detecting fraudulent activities, identifying anomalies in data sets or diagnosing system failures. One-class SVM, Isolated Forest, and Autoencoders are popular methods for outlier detection.
- **Learning Association Rules:** Learning association rules identifies interesting relationships or patterns between variables in large data sets. It is often used in market basket analysis, where the goal is to find relationships or dependencies between products that are often purchased together. Apriori and FP growth algorithms are widely used to learn association rules. Unsupervised learning has a wide range of applications in various fields, including data mining, image and text analysis, recommendation systems, and natural language processing. It enables the exploration and discovery of patterns in unstructured or unlabeled data, providing valuable insights and enabling better decisions.

The table 1 provides an overview of each learning style's essential traits and primary objectives. Unsupervised learning finds patterns in unlabelled data, supervised learning learns from labelled data to generate predictions or judgements, and reinforcement learning focuses on learning through interaction. Each variety has distinct advantages, drawbacks, and uses across a range of industries.

Table 1: Comparison of Reinforcement Learning, Supervised Learning, and Unsupervised Learning

Type	Learning Approach	Labelled Data Required?	Main Tasks
Reinforcement Learning	Learn through interaction with an environment to maximize rewards	No	Sequential decision-making, game playing, robotics
Supervised Learning	Learn from labelled data to make predictions or decisions	Yes	Classification, regression
Unsupervised Learning	Learn from unlabelled data to discover patterns or relationships	No	Clustering, dimensionality reduction

1.4. MACHINE LEARNING'S DEPENDENCE ON DATA

One of the critical factors that affect the success of machine learning algorithms is the quality and quantity of data used for training. Machine learning models learn patterns and make predictions based on information in the training data. Therefore, the availability and characteristics of the data directly affect the performance and reliability of the models. Let's explore machine learning's reliance on data and explore the topic further.

Amount of Data

The amount of data used to train machine learning models is crucial. In general, larger datasets provide more representative and diverse samples of the background population, allowing models to learn more accurately. With more data, models can capture a wider range of patterns and generalize better to unseen cases.

However, the relationship between data volume and model performance can vary depending on the complexity of the problem and the algorithm used. In some cases, even relatively small datasets can provide satisfactory results, while other tasks, especially those involving high-dimensional data or complex models, may require significantly larger datasets. In order to achieve the best possible performance of the model, it is necessary to find a balance between the available resources and the amount of data. Data quality:

The quality of information is as important as its quantity. Clean, accurate and reliable data is essential for training models that produce meaningful and reliable results. Poor data quality can lead to biased, incorrect or misleading models. Regarding the quality of information, the following factors must be considered:

5. **Data integrity:** Data integrity refers to the accuracy, completeness and consistency of data. Inaccurate or incomplete data can negatively affect the performance of machine learning models.
6. **Data preprocessing:** Preprocessing steps such as handling missing values, handling outliers and data normalization are necessary to ensure that the data is in a suitable form for training models. Proper preprocessing can improve the robustness and accuracy of models.
7. **Data bias:** Data bias can occur when training data is not representative or biased toward specific populations, groups, or characteristics. Biased information can lead to biased patterns that perpetuate unfair or discriminatory decision-making. Addressing and mitigating data distortions is critical for ethical and unbiased machine learning. Let's look at a hypothetical example to highlight machine learning's reliance on data.

Let's say we want to build a machine learning model to predict customer turnover for a telecommunications company. We collect a database consisting of customer data such as age, gender, usage patterns and service history. The dataset also includes a target variable indicating whether or not the client is experiencing difficulties. This dataset allows us to train a supervised learning model to predict customer turnover based on input characteristics. The model learns from patterns in the data and generalizes to make predictions about new, unseen customer data.

Table 2: Impact of Data Quantity and Quality on Model Performance

Aspect	Impact on Model Performance
Data Quantity	- Larger datasets provide more representative samples
	- More data helps models capture a wider range of patterns
	- Can lead to better generalization and improved model performance
Data Quality	- Accurate and reliable data is essential for meaningful results
	- Poor data quality can result in biased or erroneous models
	- Data preprocessing enhances model robustness and accuracy
	- Addressing data bias ensures fairness and unbiased predictions

Pictures

The following images illustrate the impact of data quantity and quality on model performance.

- **Amount of data and model performance:** The amount of data used for training a machine learning model and its impact on model performance is a crucial aspect of developing successful AI systems. In general, having more data can often lead to better model performance, but there are several factors to consider when evaluating the relationship between data quantity and model performance.
- **Training Data Size:** The size of the training dataset refers to the number of samples or observations available for model training. As the training data size increases, models can capture more diverse patterns and make more accurate predictions. This is because a larger dataset provides a broader representation of the underlying population or distribution, reducing the chances of overfitting (when a model memorizes the training data instead of learning generalizable patterns). However, there are diminishing returns to scale, and the performance gains tend to plateau or increase only marginally beyond a certain point.
- **Feature Representation:** The quality and richness of the features (input variables) present in the dataset are crucial for model performance. Having more data can help capture a wider range of features, especially when the dataset exhibits natural variations and includes different contexts, scenarios, or classes. More data can also help in dealing with rare events or edge cases, enabling the model to learn from such instances and make more accurate predictions.
- **Data Diversity:** The diversity of the data influences the generalization ability of the model. When the training data covers a wide range of scenarios, demographics, or contexts, the model becomes more robust and less prone to biases. By including diverse samples, the model can learn to make accurate predictions across various subgroups, reducing the risk of bias or discrimination.
- **Data Quality:** The quality of the training data is equally important as its quantity. Clean, reliable, and properly labeled data can significantly enhance model performance. Noisy or erroneous data can introduce biases, mislead the learning process, and negatively impact the model's ability to generalize. Therefore, it's crucial to ensure data quality through thorough preprocessing, data cleaning, and validation procedures.

- **Model Complexity:** The complexity of the machine learning model also plays a role in determining the impact of data quantity on performance. More complex models, such as deep neural networks, typically require larger amounts of data to learn effectively. These models have a high capacity to capture intricate patterns but are also prone to overfitting, especially when trained on limited data. Simpler models, on the other hand, may achieve satisfactory performance even with smaller datasets.
- **Domain and Task:** The impact of data quantity on model performance can vary depending on the specific domain and task. Some tasks may require vast amounts of data to achieve high performance, such as computer vision tasks that benefit from large image datasets. In contrast, other tasks, such as certain reinforcement learning problems, can achieve strong performance with smaller datasets through the use of techniques like simulation or data augmentation.

Data Quality and Model Performance

Data quality and model performance are important considerations for any machine learning project. The quality of data used to train a model directly affects its performance and ability to make accurate predictions or decisions. In this context, data quality refers to the reliability, completeness, accuracy and significance of the data used in model training and evaluation.

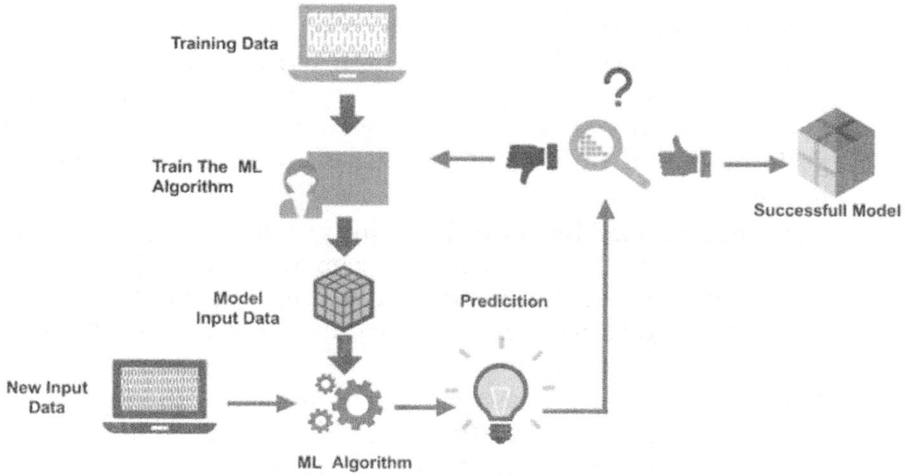

Data Quality Management

Here is a more detailed description of data quality and how it relates to model performance.

- **Reliability:** Reliable information is consistent and reliable, free from errors and inconsistencies. Data reliability ensures that the model can learn patterns and make predictions based on accurate data. On the other hand, unreliable information can lead to incorrect or misleading models.
- **Completeness:** Complete information contains all the information needed for this task. Missing or incomplete data can negatively affect a model's ability to generalize and make accurate predictions. Techniques such as imputation can be used to fill in missing values, but should be applied carefully to avoid bias.
- **Accuracy:** Accurate data is free from errors, noise and outliers. Incorrect or noisy data can mislead the model during training and affect its ability to generalize to new data. Data cleaning and preprocessing techniques are often used to identify and process inaccurate data points.
- **Relevance:** Relevant information directly related to the problem solved and related to the target domain. Irrelevant or extraneous data can introduce noise and degrade model performance. Feature selection or dimensionality reduction techniques can help remove irrelevant information and improve model performance.

Ensuring data quality directly affects the performance of machine learning models.

- **Model Training:** High quality data is very important to train accurate and reliable models. When models are taught about clean, reliable, and relevant data, they can learn meaningful patterns, relationships, and representations. This improves the performance of the model in both the training and inference phases.
- **Generalization:** Models trained on high quality data are more likely to generalize to highly unseen data. By learning from representative and unbiased data, the model can capture underlying patterns and make accurate predictions based on new real-world examples.
- **Resilience:** Robust models are immune to fluctuations or noise in the input data. If the training data is of high quality, the model is better able to handle unexpected or ambiguous scenarios, resulting in more robust and reliable performance.

- **Bias and fairness:** Data quality plays a critical role in combating biases and ensuring fairness in machine learning models. Biased or unfair data can perpetuate and reinforce existing biases, leading to discriminatory predictions or decisions. By carefully curating high-quality data and addressing biases, models can be more equal and unbiased.

It is important to note that data quality is an ongoing process. As new data becomes available or the model evolves, continuous monitoring, evaluation and improvement of data quality is necessary to maintain and improve the performance of machine learning models.

2

Fraud Detection and Anomaly Detection

2.1. INTRODUCTION TO ANOMALY DETECTION

Anomaly detection is a machine learning technique that focuses on finding observations or patterns within a dataset that significantly differ from the expected behaviour. These variations, which are also known as anomalies or outliers, can offer important information in a number of fields, such as fraud detection, network security, medical diagnostics, and industrial monitoring.

Let's examine some fundamental ideas and approaches frequently applied in this discipline in order to better comprehend anomaly detection.

Types of Anomalies

In machine learning, anomalies refer to data points or instances that deviate significantly from the norm or expected behavior. These deviations, also called outliers, can be caused by a number of factors, such as data collection errors, measurement noise, or true rare events. Detecting and understanding anomalies is an important task in many industries, including finance, cybersecurity, healthcare and manufacturing.

Machine learning can have various biases. One type is point outliers, where individual data points are considered outliers. These points may have extreme values or fall outside the range of most data. Point outliers are relatively easy to detect because they can be detected by comparing individual data points to a threshold or statistical metric.

Another type of anomaly is conte x tual anomalies. Context anomalies occur when the abnormal behavior depends on the context or combination of attributes, not just individual values. For example, a sudden rise in temperature may not be considered unusual in summer, but may be unusual in winter. To identify contextual anomalies, it is necessary to identify dependencies and relationships between different properties or attributes of the data.

Collective anomalies, also called group anomalies, contain a collection of data points that together exhibit abnormal behavior. These abnormalities are difficult to detect because they may appear normal when viewed individually, but stand out when analyzed together. An example of collective anomalies is a sharp decline in the stock prices of several companies in a certain industry. Detecting such anomalies often requires consideration of interactions and dependencies between multiple data points. Finally, temporal anomalies refer to deviations that occur over time. These anomalies include patterns or behaviors that deviate from an expected temporal sequence or trend. For example, a sudden spike in internet traffic or a significant drop in website visits can be timing anomalies. To identify temporal anomalies, it is necessary to analyze temporal data and identify deviations from expected patterns or trends.

In general, anomaly detection in machine learning is a crucial task to identify unusual or potentially valuable knowledge in various domains. Different types of anomalies require different detection methods and algorithms to effectively identify and interpret abnormal data behavior.

Anomaly Detection Techniques

Anomaly detection is a crucial task in machine learning that involves identifying unusual patterns or anomalies in data. It plays an important role in various fields, including fraud detection, network security, medical diagnostics and manufacturing quality control. Anomaly detection techniques aim to automatically identify data points that deviate significantly from normal behavior or expected patterns.

There are several approaches to outlier detection in machine learning. One common technique is a statistical approach that assumes normal data points follow a known distribution. Statistical methods such as Gaussian distribution modeling, z-score calculation, and percentile ranking can be used to identify data points that fall outside the expected range.

Another approach is based on machine learning algorithms. These methods involve training a model on a named data set where normals and outliers are clearly defined. The model learns patterns of normal behavior and can then classify new cases as either normal or abnormal. Popular machine learning algorithms for outlier detection include k-nearest neighbors (KNN), support vector machines (SVM), and isolation forests. Clustering algorithms can also be used to detect anomalies. These methods group similar data points together, assuming that outliers form clear clusters or fall into small sparse groups. Events that do not belong to any cluster or are assigned to small clusters are considered extraordinary.

In recent years, deep learning approaches have gained attention in anomaly detection. Deep autoencoders, generative adversarial networks (GANs), and recurrent neural networks (RNNs) can learn complex representations of data and detect anomalies based on reconstruction error or deviation from learned patterns. Feature design and selection are critical to anomaly detection. The selection of relevant features and preprocessing steps can significantly affect the performance of anomaly detection algorithms. Domain knowledge and expertise play an important role in identifying significant features and designing effective anomaly detection systems.

Evaluating outlier detection techniques is difficult because data sets typically have an unbalanced class distribution and outliers are in the minority. Common evaluation measures include precision, recall, F1 score, and area under the receiver operating curve (AUC-ROC). In general, machine learning anomaly detection techniques use statistical, machine learning, clustering and deep learning methods to detect unusual data. These techniques are constantly evolving due to the availability of algorithms, feature design, and large-scale labeled datasets, enabling more accurate and efficient anomaly detection in various real-world applications.

Evaluation Metrics

Evaluation metrics are important tools used to evaluate the effectiveness and efficiency of machine learning models. These metrics provide objective metrics to help evaluate how well a model performs in its predictions and its ability to generalize to unseen data. By quantifying model performance, evaluation metrics enable researchers and practitioners to compare different models, select the model best suited for a particular task, and identify areas for improvement.

Various evaluation metrics are available, and the choice of metric depends on the nature of the problem being solved and the specific goals of the machine learning task. Some commonly used evaluation metrics are precision, accuracy, recall, F1 score, and area under the curve (AUC). Accuracy is a widely used metric that measures the total accuracy of the predictions of a model, expressed as the ratio of correctly classified cases to the total number of cases. However, accuracy alone may not give the full picture, especially when dealing with unbalanced datasets where classes are not equally represented.

Precision and recall are commonly used metrics in binary classification tasks. Precision measures the proportion of true positive predictions out of all predicted positives, while recall measures the proportion of true positives out of all true positives. Precision focuses on the ability of the model to minimize false positives, while recall emphasizes the ability to minimize false positives. The F1 score is a harmonic mean of precision and recall, providing a balanced measure of model performance considering both precision and recall. This is particularly useful if there is an imbalance between positive and negative events in the dataset.

AUC is a metric used to evaluate the performance of models in binary classification tasks based on their receiver operating characteristic (ROC) curve. The ROC curve plots the true positive rate (TPR) as a function of the false positive rate (FPR) at different classification thresholds. AUC represents the area under this curve and measures the ability of the model to distinguish between positive and negative cases. In addition to these commonly used metrics, there are domain specific metrics that are tailored for specific tasks. For example, object detection tasks typically use mean accuracy (mAP), while regression tasks use mean square error (MSE) and root mean square error (RMSE).

Visualization Techniques

Machine learning visualization techniques refer to various methods and tools used to visually represent and analyze complex data and patterns. As the complexity and interpretability of machine learning algorithms grows in importance, visualization plays a critical role in understanding and communicating insights from models.

One common visualization technique is data visualization, which involves creating graphical representations of input data. It allows analysts and data scientists to explore patterns, trends and relationships in a data set. Methods such as scatterplots, histograms, heatmaps, and boxplots provide visual cues to help identify outliers, clusters, and correlations, aiding in informed decisions about data processing, feature design, and model selection. Another important aspect of visualization in machine learning is model visualization. This involves creating visual representations of the inner workings of machine learning models so that users can gain insight into how the models make predictions. For example, decision trees can be visualized as hierarchical structures that describe the decision process of each node. This visualization helps to understand the logic and rules used in the model.

In addition, visualization techniques are used to interpret model outputs, especially in complex models such as deep neural networks. Activation maps and saliency maps are visualizations that highlight important regions of the input image that influence the model's prediction. These techniques provide insight into the focus of the model and help identify potential biases or areas for improvement.

Also, the visualization helps to evaluate the performance of the model and evaluate the effectiveness of different algorithms or hyperparameters. ROC curves, accuracy normalization curves, and confusion matrices are commonly used visualizations that provide a comprehensive view of model performance for various evaluation metrics. These visualizations make it easy to compare models and help choose the most appropriate algorithm or configuration. In addition, interactive visualizations are increasingly common in machine learning. These visualizations allow users to interact with data and models, allowing them to explore different scenarios, adjust parameters and observe real-time changes. Interactive visualizations foster a deeper understanding of the underlying concepts and encourage collaboration between stakeholders.

In conclusion, machine learning visualization techniques are essential for understanding, interpreting and communicating insights from complex data and models. Using visual representations, analysts and data scientists can discover hidden patterns, gain insights into model behavior, evaluate performance, and make informed decisions during machine learning.

In conclusion, anomaly detection is an essential component of machine learning that is used to spot odd patterns or occurrences in a dataset. Anomalies can be found using a variety of approaches and visualisation methods, allowing organisations to reduce risks, spot fraud, and make sure that processes and systems are running smoothly.

2.2 STATISTICAL APPROACHES FOR ANOMALY DETECTION

Finding patterns or occurrences within a dataset that significantly vary from expected behaviour is known as anomaly detection in machine learning. The underlying statistical features of the data are used in statistical approaches for anomaly detection to identify anomalies using a variety of statistical techniques.

Z-Score or Standard Deviation Method

Both Z-score and standard deviation methods are used as characteristic scaling and normalization techniques in machine learning, especially when dealing with numerical data. The purpose of these methods is to transform the data into a common scale to ensure a fair comparison and prevent specific characteristics from dominating the learning process.

The z-score method, also known as standardization, calculates the number of standard deviations a data point is away from the mean. It subtracts the trait mean from each data point and then divides the result by the trait standard deviation. This process ensures that the transformed data has a mean of 0 and a standard deviation of 1. The formula for calculating the Z-score of a data point x is: (x - mean) / standard deviation.

Standardization using the Z-score method is useful when the distribution of features is approximately normal or Gaussian. This helps handle outliers and ensures that the functions have a comparable scale, which is useful for algorithms based on distance calculations or optimizations.

The standard deviation method, on the other hand, simply scales the data by dividing each data point by the characteristic standard deviation. The scaling formula for standard deviation is: x / standard deviation. This method does not center the data around zero like the Z-score method, but instead adjusts the scale of the function based on its variability.

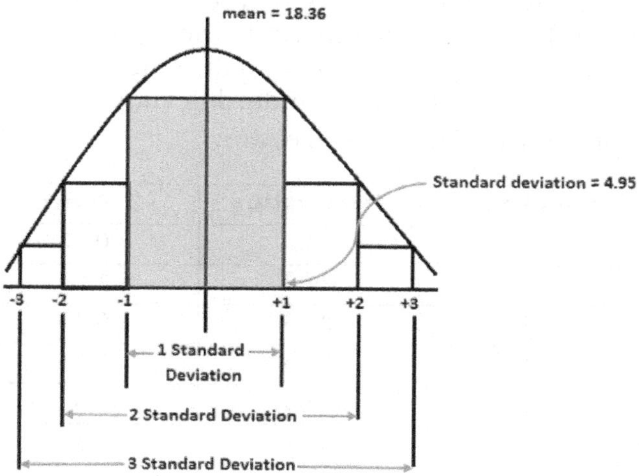

Z-Score or Standard Deviation Method

The choice between the Z-score and the standard deviation method depends on the specific requirements of the machine learning problem at hand. If maintaining the mean and achieving a standard deviation of 1 is important, the Z-score method is preferable. However, if it is not necessary to keep the original mean and simply scaling by the standard deviation is sufficient, the standard deviation method can be used.

Both methods play an important role in ensuring proper scaling and normalization of properties, which can lead to better model performance, faster convergence, and better generalization. It is important to apply these techniques in the preprocessing phase of machine learning pipelines to ensure a fair and accurate comparison of features and facilitate optimal learning by algorithms.

Example:

Consider the following dataset of temperature readings:

Data Point	Temperature
1	23.5
2	24.2
3	23.8
4	25.5
5	23.3
6	28.9

We determine the mean and standard deviation of the temperature readings in order to use the z-score method to identify abnormalities. Assume that 24.0 is the mean and 1.5 is the standard deviation. With the help of the following equation, we can determine the z-score for each data point: z = (x - mean) / standard deviation.

The z-scores for the given dataset are:

Data Point	Temperature	Z-Score
1	23.5	-0.33
2	24.2	0.13
3	23.8	-0.13
4	25.5	1.00
5	23.3	-0.47
6	28.9	2.60

Modified Z-Score Method

The modified Z-score method is a statistical technique commonly used in machine learning to detect outliers in a dataset. An outlier is an observation that deviates significantly from the general pattern or distribution of data points. Deviations can create noise in the model and impair its performance. The modified Z-Score method provides a systematic approach to identifying and dealing with such outliers.

The method begins by calculating Z-scores for each data point in the dataset. The z-score measures how many standard deviations a given data point is away from the mean of the data set. However, the standard Z-score has some limitations, especially when dealing with data that is not normally distributed or contains extreme values. Therefore, the modified Z-score method addresses these limitations by using the mean absolute deviation (MAD) as a robust measure of variance.

To calculate the modified Z-score, we first calculate the median (M) and mean absolute deviation (MAD) of the data set. MAD is the median of the absolute differences for each data point and the median of the data set. We then calculate the modified Z-score (MZ) for each data point using the following formula:

MZ = 0.6745* (X - M) / MAD

Here, X represents each data point in the dataset. The default value of 0.6745 is used to ensure that the MZ values are as consistent as the standard Z-score.

Once the MZ values are calculated, we can set a threshold to detect outliers. A common threshold value is 3.5, which suggests that any data point with an MZ value greater than 3.5 or less than -3.5 is considered an outlier. However, the threshold can be adjusted based on the special characteristics of the data set and the desired sensitivity to outliers. Once identified, abnormalities can be treated in a number of different ways. One option is to completely remove outliers from the dataset. This approach may be appropriate when deviations are considered erroneous or unrelated to the problem at hand. Another approach is to replace the outliers with a more representative value, such as the median or mean of the data set. This approach can help maintain a shared distribution and prevent valuable information from being lost. In conclusion, the modified Z-score method provides a robust statistical technique for outlier detection and use in machine learning. By using the absolute mean deviation, it overcomes the limitations of the standard Z-Score method and provides a more reliable measure of variance. Embedding this method into machine learning pipelines can improve model performance and provide more accurate and reliable predictions.

Example:

Consider the following dataset of response times (in milliseconds) for a web server:

Data Point	Response Time
1	50
2	55
3	54
4	52
5	5000
6	53

We determine the median and MAD of the response times in order to use the modified z-score approach to identify abnormalities. Assume that the MAD is 1.4826 and the median is 53.5. Each data point's updated z-score can be determined.

The modified z-scores for the given dataset are:

Data Point	Response Time	Modified Z-Score
1	50	-2.02
2	55	0.34
3	54	-0.34
4	52	-1.02
5	5000	2124.64
6	53	-0.68

2.3. CLUSTERING-BASED ANOMALY DETECTION

A machine learning technique called clustering-based anomaly detection is used to find and recognise odd patterns or outliers in datasets. It entails assembling clusters of related data points and spotting those that significantly depart from the cluster's predicted behaviour.

Data Pre-processing

Data pre-processing is a key step in machine learning, where raw data is transformed into a clean and structured form suitable for analysis and model training. It is an integral part of the data pipeline and greatly affects the performance and accuracy of machine learning algorithms.

The goal of data processing is to resolve common data problems such as missing values, outliers, inconsistencies, and noise that can negatively affect learning. Various pre-processing techniques can make data more reliable, consistent, and suitable for training predictive models.

One of the first steps in data pre-processing is data cleaning, in which missing values are handled, for example by imputation or deletion. Missing values can cause bias and affect the overall quality of the data, so appropriate strategies are used to fill or remove these gaps. In the same way, deviations that are significantly different from the rest of the data are identified and corrected or removed.

Another important aspect of data processing is data normalization or scaling. This requires converting the numerical properties of the data to a standardized range, typically between 0 and 1 or -1 and 1. Scaling is necessary to ensure that different scale or unit properties do not dominate the learning, as many machine learning algorithms are sensitive. to the scale of the input data. Categorical data representing discrete values, such as colors or categories, must be encoded in numerical form to be processed by machine learning algorithms. This can be achieved using methods such as one-hot coding, where each class is converted to a binary function, or tag coding, which assigns a unique numerical identifier to each class.

Feature selection or dimensionality reduction is another important step in data processing. It identifies and selects the most important features that significantly affect the target variable and discards those that are pale or unnecessary. This helps reduce computational complexity, improve model efficiency, and avoid the curse of dimensionality. In addition, data processing can also include handling skewed distributions, transforming nonlinear relationships, and handling class imbalances in classification tasks. These techniques aim to improve data quality, improve model interpretability, and provide better generalization to unseen data.

Transaction ID	Amount	Time	Location
1	100	9AM	A
2	50	2PM	B
3	200	3PM	C
4	300	6PM	A
5	75	8AM	B

2.4. SUPPORT VECTOR MACHINES (SVM) FOR ANOMALY DETECTION

Support vector machines (SVM) can be used in machine learning to detect outliers. Anomaly detection means identifying data points or patterns that differ significantly from normal or expected behavior. SVMs that can capture complex decision constraints can effectively discriminate between normal and abnormal data points.

For the SVM anomaly detection workflow:

A general workflow for using SVM for anomaly detection typically includes the following steps.

- **Step 1:** Data preprocessing
- **Step 2:** Remove the function
- **Step 3:** Train the SVM on the normal data
- **Step 4:** Detection of anomalies
- **Step 5:** Evaluation of Anomaly Detection Performance

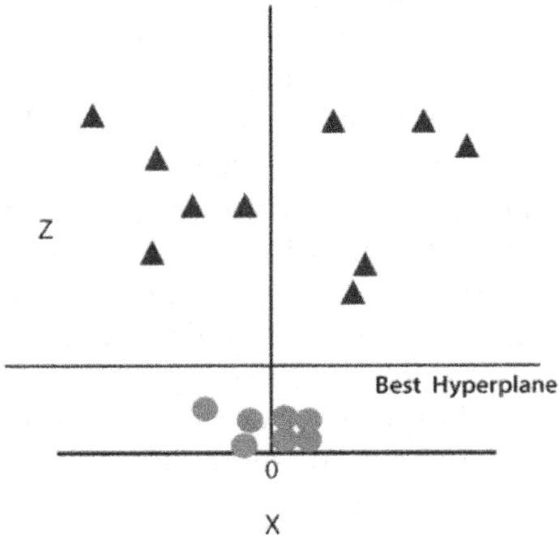

Support Vector Machines (SVM) Algorithm

Data Preprocessing

Data preprocessing is a key step in machine learning, where raw data is converted into a format suitable for analysis and modeling. This is a fundamental step in general machine learning and greatly affects the efficiency and accuracy of the resulting models. The primary purpose of data preprocessing is to clean, normalize, and reorganize data to ensure consistency, completeness, and relevance.

The data processing process involves several techniques and steps. First, data cleaning is performed to correct missing values, outliers, and inconsistent data. Missing values can be imputed using different methods such as mean, median or mode replacement, or more complex techniques such as regression or multiple imputation. Outliers, which are extreme values that differ significantly from the rest of the data, can be handled, for example, by trimming, scoring, or removing outliers altogether.

Another important aspect of data processing is data normalization or scaling. This step ensures that all features have a similar range and distribution, which helps algorithms converge faster and prevents some features from dominating others. Common normalization techniques include min-max scaling, where values are transformed to a specific range, and standardization, where data are transformed so that their mean and unit variance are zero. In addition, categorical variables must be coded as numerical values, which are processed using machine learning algorithms. This process, called feature coding or feature transformation, is typically done using techniques such as one-hot coding, where each category is converted into a separate binary feature, or tag coding, where each category is assigned a numerical identifier.

Additionally, feature selection or dimensionality reduction methods can be used to reduce the number of features while keeping the most informative ones. Methods such as principal component analysis (PCA) or feature ranking can help identify the most important features, reducing computational complexity and avoiding overfitting.

Finally, data processing involves dividing the dataset into training, validation and test sets. The training set is used to train the machine learning model, the validation set is used to set the hyperparameters and evaluate the performance of the model, while the test set serves to unbiasedly evaluate the final model.

Feature Extraction

Characterization is a critical process in machine learning where raw data is transformed into a representation that captures relevant information for a learning algorithm. Its purpose is to identify and extract the most informative features from the input data, which can be in different formats such as images, text or numerical data. By selecting the right features, feature extraction simplifies the subsequent learning process and improves the overall performance of the machine learning model.

The feature extraction process usually involves several steps. First, raw data are processed to remove noise, normalize values and handle missing data, if any. Next, domain-specific knowledge and expertise are used to identify important features that are likely to have a significant impact on the learning process. This can involve understanding the underlying problem, examining the data, and using past data to select features.

Once an initial set of potential features has been identified, various techniques are used to obtain meaningful information. For images, this may involve using filters, edge detection or other image processing techniques to extract important visual features. Text data can use techniques such as tokenization, derivation and vectorization to transform the text into a numerical representation that captures semantic information. Statistical measures and mathematical transformations can be used to identify significant patterns and relationships in numerical data.

Feature extraction plays a crucial role in machine learning because it helps reduce the dimensionality of data and removes pale or redundant features that can cause overfitting or poor generalization. By presenting the data in a more compact and informative way, it allows the machine learning algorithm to focus on the most characteristic aspects of the data, resulting in better model performance and faster computation. Moreover, feature splitting can help deal with the curse of dimensionality by reducing the number of features and thereby improving computational efficiency.

Training SVM on Normal Data

Support Vector Machines (SVM) is a popular machine learning supervised learning algorithm that can be used for both classification and regression tasks. Training an SVM on normal data means that the data used for training represents the normal behavior or class of the dataset.

The goal of SVM is to find the optimal hyperplane that separates the classes or categories of different data points. For normal data, the goal of SVM is to create a decision boundary that effectively separates normal cases from abnormal or abnormal cases. The training process involves finding a hyperplane that maximizes the margin or distance between the decision boundary of each class and the nearest data points. Training an SVM on normal data requires a labeled dataset, where each case is associated with a class label indicating whether it is normal or abnormal. The training data should contain a sufficient number of examples representative of the normal class. The SVM algorithm then learns from these frequent events to create a model that can accurately classify new events as normal or abnormal based on their characteristic values.

In the training phase, the SVM algorithm optimizes the cost function by adjusting the hyperplane parameters. The goal of this optimization process is to minimize classification errors and maximize the margin between the decision boundary and the support vectors closest to the decision boundary. By finding the optimal hyperplane, SVM can generalize well to new, never-before-seen cases and effectively distinguish normal data from abnormal data.

After SVM is trained on normal data, it can be used to classify new cases and detect outliers based on their feature values. The trained model can assign to each new case a class label indicating whether it is normal or abnormal according to the learned decision boundary.

Training an SVM on regular data is crucial for several applications such as fraud detection, network intrusion detection, and anomaly detection. By accurately modeling normal behavior, SVMs can effectively detect deviations from normal patterns that may indicate anomalies, intrusions, or fraudulent activity. It is important to note that the performance of SVM in abnormal or non-normal cases depends greatly on the quality and representativeness of the training data, as well as the choice of appropriate hyperparameters and the overall modeling process.

Detecting Anomalies

Anomaly detection in machine learning is a critical task that involves identifying and flagging data points or patterns that significantly deviate from normal or expected behavior. Anomalies, also known as anomalies or novelties, can be caused by a number of reasons, such as data collection errors, system failures, fraudulent activities or rare events. Anomaly detection aims to distinguish those abnormal cases from the majority of data representing normal behavior.

There are several ways to identify machine learning anomalies. One common method is statistical outlier detection, which analyzes the statistical properties of the data and identifies cases that fall outside a defined interval or have a low probability in a given statistical distribution. This approach assumes that outliers have distinct statistical properties that differ from the bulk of the data.

Another approach is machine learning-based anomaly detection, which uses techniques such as supervised or unsupervised learning algorithms. In supervised learning, identified training data is used to train a model that can classify cases as normal or abnormal. In contrast, unsupervised learning attempts to learn the underlying structure of the data without explicit identifiers and can identify outliers as data points that do not conform to learned patterns.

In recent years, deep learning techniques, especially neural networks, have shown promising results in anomaly detection. Autoencoders, a type of neural network architecture, are often used to detect uncontrolled anomalies. They are trained to accurately reconstruct normal phenomena, and any differences between the input and the reconstructed output are considered anomalies.

In addition to algorithmic approaches, anomaly detection is also based on feature planning, data preprocessing, and domain knowledge. Feature engineering involves selecting or creating meaningful features that can effectively capture the characteristics of common and unusual cases. Data processing techniques such as scaling, normalization, or outlier removal can improve the performance of outlier detection algorithms. Domain knowledge is critical for understanding the context of the data and defining outliers in a particular area.

Evaluating Anomaly Detection Performance

Anomaly detection evaluation in machine learning evaluates the effectiveness of algorithms or models in detecting and flagging unusual or abnormal occurrences in a dataset. Anomaly detection is a critical task in many fields, including cyber security, fraud detection, industrial quality control, and system monitoring.

Several metrics are commonly used to evaluate the performance of an anomaly detection system. One of the most important metrics is the confusion matrix, which gives an idea of the system's ability to classify cases as normal or abnormal. The confusion matrix includes metrics such as true positives (correctly detecte d anomalies), true negatives (correctly detected normal cases), fals e positives (normal cases incorrectly labeled as anomalies), and false negatives (outliers ignored by the system). Another relevant metric is the receiver operating characteristic (ROC) curve, which describes the trade-off between true positive rate (sensitivity or recall) and false positive rate (specificity) at different threshold values. Area under the ROC cu rve (AUC-ROC) is often used as a summary measure when comparing di fferent outlier detection models. A higher AUC-ROC value means be t ter overall performance.

Precision, recall, and F1 score are also commonly used metrics to evaluate outlier detection performance. Precision measures the proportion of correctly identified outliers out of all cases classified as anomalies, while recall measures the proportion of correctly identified outliers out of all true outliers. The F1 score combines precision and recall into a single metric that provides a balanced assessment of model performance.

In addition, for certain applications, it may be necessary to perform area-specific evaluation measures. For example, in fraud detection, a metric such as average accuracy K (AP@K) or a spike plot can be used to evaluate the model's ability to prioritize the detection of value anomalies.

In addition to these metrics, visualizations such as accuracy recovery plots, detection rate plots, or cumulative gain plots can provide additional insight into the performance characteristics of anomaly detection models.

2.5. ISOLATION FOREST FOR ANOMALY DETECTION

Popular machine learning algorithm for anomaly identification is isolation forest. It uses the idea of separating anomalies from the typical instances in a dataset and is a tree-based technique. By creating isolation trees, the programme efficiently finds anomalies.

Isolation Forest Algorithm

The isolated forest algorithm is a powerful machine learning technique used for anomaly detection and anomaly detection. It is based on isolating anomalies rather than identifying normal cases. The algorithm developed by Liu, Ting, and Zhou in 2008 offers several advantages, including the ability to handle large-scale data sets, efficiency in processing large data sets, and sensitivity to data size and distribution.

The idea behind the isolated forest algorithm revolves around the observation that anomalies are often located in sparse regions of the data space. The algorithm creates a set of splitting trees, which are binary trees constructed by randomly selecting features and partitioning the data by those features. The partitioning process continues recursively until individual instances are isolated or a given maximum tree depth is reached.

When building isolation trees, anomalies have a higher probability of isolation earlier in the tree structure than normal cases. This is because outliers are more likely to be separated by a random partitioning process. On the other hand, normal instances require more partitioning steps to separate them because they are tightly packed.

However, like any algorithm, Isolation Forest has its limitations. It can struggle with data sets with a large number of outliers, or when the outliers occur in densely populated areas of the data. In addition, determining the optimal threshold for reporting anomalies can be difficult and may require domain expertise or additional analysis.

In conclusion, the Isolated Forest algorithm provides an efficient and effective approach for outlier detection. Using the concept of outlier extraction, it provides a robust solution to detect outliers in various domains, making it a valuable tool in the field of machine learning and data analysis.

Isolation Trees

Isolated trees, also known as isolation forests, are a popular machine learning technique used for anomaly detection and anomaly detection. They allow the identification of observations that differ significantly from the usual patterns in the data. The basic idea of isolation trees is to isolate outliers by building binary trees and measuring their average isolation depth.

Creating an isolation tree requires recursively partitioning the dataset into smaller subsets until isolation is achieved. At each step, a random feature and a random cutoff point are selected to split the data. This process continues until the algorithm reaches a predefined stopping criterion, such as the maximum depth of the tree or the minimum number of samples at a leaf node.

External isolation is determined based on the depth of the data point of the established trees. The average path length of normal events is expected to be shorter than that of abnormal events. During the tree construction process, if a case reaches a leaf node in only a few samples, it is more likely to be outlier. Therefore, the average path length for each data point to reach a leaf node is a measure of its anomaly. For outlier detection, isolation scores for each data point are calculated based on its average path length across multiple trees. The higher the score, the more likely the point is extraordinary. By setting a threshold, observations with a score higher than this can be classified as outliers.

Isolation trees have several advantages. They are computationally efficient, especially for high-dimensional data sets, because they can operate with linear time complexity. They are also robust to outliers and require no assumptions about the underlying data distribution. In addition, spanning trees can handle different data types and are not affected by irrelevant properties.

An example of an isolation tree is shown below:

Node (Split on feature X2)

```
         /        \
   Node (Split on feature X1)  Leaf (Instance 1)
      /      \
 Leaf (Instance 2)  Leaf (Instance 3)
```

Path Length

Path length is a concept that plays an important role in various machine learning algorithms, especially decision trees and random forests. It refers to the number of edges transported from the root node of a given decision tree to a given leaf node. The length of the path provides valuable information about the complexity and interpretability of the model.

In addition, the path length affects the training and prediction times of the model. Shorter paths lead to faster predictions because fewer feature estimates are required. On the other hand, longer paths increase computational complexity, especially when dealing with large data sets or deep decision trees.

Random forests, an ensemble learning method, consist of multiple decision trees. Each tree in the forest is trained on a different subset of data, and the final prediction is obtained by aggregation. In this context, the path length is important in determining object importance in a random forest model. Features that lead to shorter paths between multiple trees are often considered more influential in the overall prediction process.

In addition, the length of the road is closely related to the overlap. Decision trees with excessively long paths tend to capture noise or outliers in the training data, resulting in overfitting. Overfitting models have poor generalizability and may not accurately predict from unseen data. Control techniques such as pruning or setting maximum depth limits can be used to limit the path length and prevent overcrowding. In summary, path length is key for decision trees and random forests in machine learning. It provides insights into model complexity, interpretability, computational efficiency, feature importance, and risk of overfitting. Understanding and managing path length can have a significant impact on the effectiveness and usability of machine learning models.

Anomaly Score

Machine learning anomaly scores refer to a metric or value assigned to data points or instances that indicate the degree of deviation or deviation from expected or normal behavior in the data set. Outliers, also known as anomalies or unusual observations, can provide valuable insights and often represent important patterns or events that deviate significantly from the norm. Anomaly detection is a critical task in many fields, including fraud detection, network intrusion detection, system monitoring, and quality control.

Anomaly scores are typically calculated based on the characteristics of data points or features and the model used to detect anomalies. It captures patterns and regularities in most data and then quantifies the deviations of individual cases from those patterns. Various machine learning techniques are used to detect anomalies, such as statistical methods, clustering algorithms, and supervised or unsupervised learning methods.

The interpretation of anomaly points depends on the specific application and the chosen anomaly detection algorithm. A higher deviance score generally indicates a greater likelihood that the case is abnormal, while a lower score indicates similarity to normal behavior. However, the exact threshold for treating a data point as an outlier is usually determined by industry expertise or attempts to balance false positives and false negatives.

Anomaly Threshold

In machine learning, a key concept used in anomaly detection tasks is the anomaly threshold. Anomaly detection refers to the process of identifying patterns or instances that deviate significantly from the norm or expected behavior of a data set. Anomaly thresholds play an important role in this process because they help distinguish between normal and abnormal cases.

It is important to note that deviation thresholds are not necessarily fixed and may adjust in certain scenarios. In dynamic environments or situations where the underlying distribution of the data changes over time, it may be necessary to change the threshold accordingly. Adaptive thresholding techniques can monitor data properties and dynamically update the threshold to accommodate such changes.

Example Anomaly Detection Results

Consider the following example of anomaly detection using the Isolation Forest algorithm:

Instance	Feature 1	Feature 2	Feature 3	Anomaly Score
1	0.6	0.8	0.7	0.23
2	0.3	0.5	0.4	0.68
3	0.2	0.7	0.9	0.19

Instance	Feature 1	Feature 2	Feature 3	Anomaly Score
4	0.1	0.2	0.3	0.71
5	0.9	0.1	0.5	0.66

The cutoff for categorising occurrences as anomalies would be 0.23 if the contamination parameter were set to 0.2 (20% anomalies). Instances 1, 3, and 4 would be categorised as anomalies based on the anomaly ratings, however instances 2 and 5 would be categorised as normal.

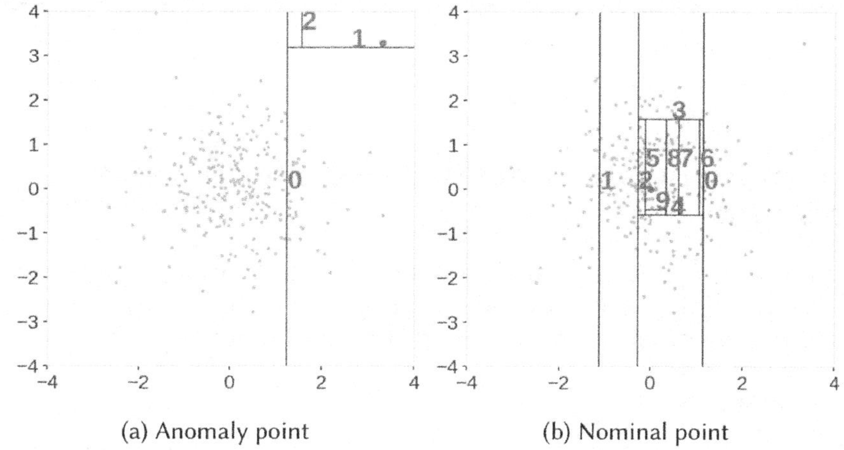

Isolation Forest for Anomaly Detection

3

Machine Learning in Healthcare

3.1. INTRODUCTION OF HEALTHCARE MACHINE LEARNING APPLICATIONS

By making it possible to create several applications that enhance patient care, diagnostic accuracy, and operational efficiency, machine learning has completely transformed the healthcare sector.

Disease Diagnosis

Machine learning disease diagnosis refers to the application of advanced computer algorithms and techniques to detect and predict various diseases. With the exponential growth of medical data and the increase of powerful computing resources, machine learning has become a valuable tool in healthcare.

Machine learning models analyze large amounts of medical data, including patient records, medical images, lab results, genetic information and clinical notes. These models use algorithms to learn patterns and relationships in the data and then make predictions or classifications based on that information. Using this information, machine learning algorithms can help with early disease detection, accurate diagnosis and personalized treatment. One of the main advantages of using machine learning in disease diagnosis is its ability to process complex and multidimensional data. Traditional diagnostic methods often rely on manual interpretation and subjective judgment, which can be time-consuming and error-prone. In contrast, machine learning models can quickly process huge amounts of data and extract relevant features that may not be obvious to human observers. This can lead to more accurate and efficient diagnoses.

Although machine learning holds promise for disease diagnosis, there are still challenges and limitations to overcome. Data protection, interpretability and ethical aspects are important factors to be addressed. In addition, the integration of machine learning models into clinical workflows and decision-making processes requires careful validation and regulatory approvals to ensure patient safety and effective healthcare.

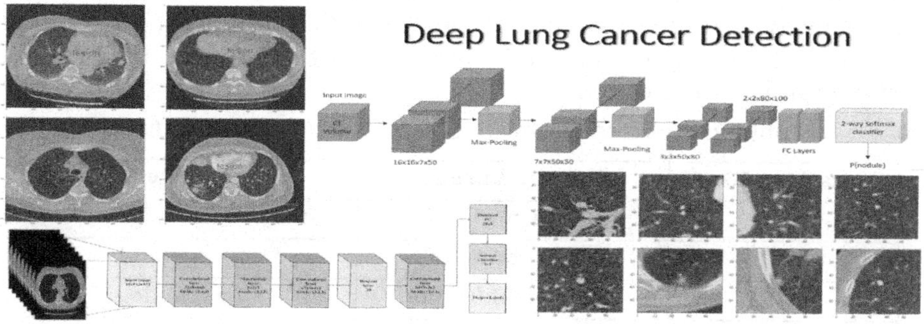

Cancer Diagnosis in ML

Table 1: Performance Comparison of Cancer Diagnosis Models

Model	Accuracy (%)	Sensitivity (%)	Specificity (%)
Convolutional Neural Networks	93.5	92.1	94.3
Support Vector Machines	89.8	88.2	91.3
Random Forest	90.2	87.6	92.5

Personalized Treatment

Personalized care in machine learning refers to the development and application of algorithms and techniques that enable personalized and individualized interventions or treatments in various domains, including healthcare, education and customer service. The concept is based on the use of large personal data, such as their characteristics, preferences and historical data, to create personalized models or systems that can predict and provide personalized recommendations, treatment or intervention.

In healthcare, personalized care has received considerable attention for its potential to revolutionize patient care. Machine learning models can help healthcare professionals identify the most appropriate treatments, medications or interventions for specific patients by analyzing individuals' genetic information, medical history, lifestyle factors and responses to previous treatments. These models can predict disease risks, optimize treatment plans and even help develop new drugs or treatments tailored to a person's unique characteristics. Individual treatment can be implemented in teaching that improves students' learning. Machine learning algorithms can analyze student performance data, learning styles and preferences to create personalized learning paths. These pathways can include customized assignments, resources, and feedback that allow students to learn at their own pace and in a way that meets their individual needs. The goal of personalized educational therapy is to improve engagement, academic achievement, and overall learning outcomes.

Table 2: Predicted Treatment Outcomes for Precision Medicine

Patient ID	Genetic Variant	Predicted Response
001	BRCA1 mutation	Responder
002	EGFR mutation	Non-responder
003	HER2 amplification	Responder
004	KRAS mutation	Non-responder

Patient Monitoring

Machine learning patient monitoring refers to the application of advanced computing techniques to collect, analyze and interpret patient health data. This involves using machine learning algorithms and models to monitor various physiological parameters such as heart rate, blood pressure, oxygen saturation and respiratory rate. These algorithms are designed to process large amounts of patient data, often obtained from wearables, sensors or medical devices, to provide real-time insights into the patient's condition.

One of the most important benefits of machine learning patient monitoring is its ability to detect subtle changes in patient health that traditional monitoring methods may miss. Machine learning algorithms can identify patterns, trends and anomalies that may indicate potential health problems or deterioration by continuously analyzing data from multiple sources. This early detection allows healthcare providers to intervene quickly, improving patient outcomes and potentially preventing serious complications.

Machine learning models used in patient monitoring can be trained on large datasets containing different patient populations and diseases. This allows algorithms to learn complex patterns and correlations that can indicate specific health conditions or predict future events. For example, machine learning models have been developed to predict the likelihood of cardiac arrest or identify patients at risk of sepsis based on their vital signs and other clinical data.

However, patient monitoring involves machine learning challenges. Ensuring data accuracy, privacy and security is critical because patient health information is very sensitive. Integrating data from different sources and standardizing formats is also important for smooth analysis and interpretation. In addition, the application of machine learning models in clinical settings requires careful validation and regulatory compliance to ensure their reliability and safety.

Table 3: Early Warning Scores for Patient Monitoring

Patient ID	Heart Rate	Blood Pressure	Respiratory Rate	Early Warning Score
001	80	120/80	18	3.5
002	110	140/90	24	8.2
003	70	110/70	16	1.8

These are only a few instances of machine learning being used in the healthcare industry. The field is broad and includes a wide range of other applications, including drug development, patient risk prediction, medical image segmentation, and resource allocation optimisation.

3.2. ELECTRONIC HEALTH RECORDS (EHR) ANALYSIS

Machine learning's discipline of Electronic Health Records (EHR) Analysis uses cutting-edge algorithms and methods to glean important patterns and insights from the enormous amounts of data kept in electronic health records. This analysis can benefit medical research while also assisting in the optimisation of healthcare procedures and patient care.

Introduction to Electronic Health Records (EHR)

Electronic health records (EHR) play a central role in modern healthcare systems, and their integration with machine learning methods could revolutionize healthcare delivery. EHR stands for a digital system that stores and manages patient health information in a secure and systematic way. It contains comprehensive information such as medical history, diagnoses, medications, laboratory results and treatment plans, making it a valuable source of information for healthcare providers. Machine learning, a subset of artificial intelligence, involves developing algorithms and models that can analyze and interpret large amounts of data to identify patterns, make predictions, and provide actionable insights. By applying machine learning algorithms to EHR data, healthcare professionals can extract meaningful information, better understand patient populations, predict disease, identify abnormalities, and support clinical decision making. Integrating machine learning into the EHR promises to improve health outcomes, improve patient safety, optimize resource allocation and ultimately improve the quality and efficiency of health services. However, challenges such as data quality, privacy concerns, and the interpretability of machine learning models must be addressed to ensure responsible and effective use of this powerful technology in healthcare settings.

Role of Machine Learning in EHR Analysis

Machine learning plays a central role in electronic health record (EHR) analysis, revolutionizing the interpretation and use of health data. EHR files contain a large amount of patient information, including medical history, diagnoses, treatment plans, lab results, and more. However, gaining meaningful insights from these complex and heterogeneous data sets can be challenging. This is where machine learning techniques come into play.

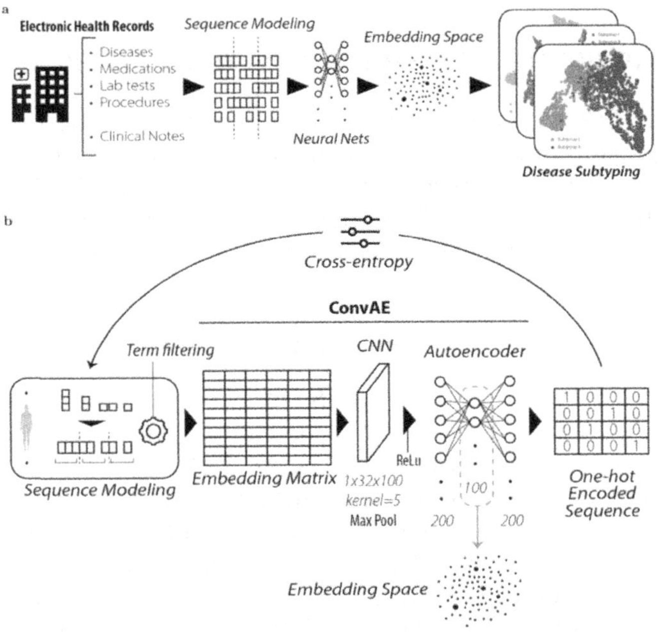

EHR Analysis

In addition, machine learning can facilitate clinical decision-making systems by providing evidence-based recommendations and guidance.

By analyzing large amounts of EHR data, machine learning models can make personalized treatment recommendations, alert healthcare providers to potential drug interactions or side effects, and help detect disease early.

In addition, machine learning techniques enable meaningful insights from unstructured EHR data such as physician notes, radiology reports, and pathology images. Natural Language Processing (NLP) algorithms combined with machine learning can analyze and interpret text data and transform it into structured information that can be used for decision making and research.

of each algorithm. Interpretability and explainability are also important issues in machine learning. As models become increasingly complex, such as deep learning neural networks, understanding the reasons behind these predictions becomes difficult. This lack of interpretability is a concern in critical sectors such as healthcare and finance, where transparent decision-making is essential. To solve this problem, the goal is to develop explainable artificial intelligence technologies that allow people to understand and trust the decisions made by machine learning models.

Ethical considerations are paramount in machine learning. Bias can come from biased training data or discriminatory models from the algorithms themselves, leading to unfair or discriminatory results. Addressing these biases requires careful review of data collection and preprocessing methods, as well as algorithm design and evaluation. Ensuring fairness, accountability and transparency in machine learning models is critical to reducing potential harm and promoting ethical decision-making.

In addition, the rapid development of technology and the need for continuous model monitoring present additional challenges. Machine learning models are not static, but evolve over time and require regular updating and retraining to maintain performance. Monitoring model degradation, conceptual drift, and unexpected behavior is essential to ensure reliable and trustworthy predictions.

Overall, machine learning offers tremendous potential, but comes with challenges and considerations that must be addressed. These include data quality and availability, choice of algorithms, interpretability, ethical considerations, and the need for ongoing model monitoring. By proactively responding to these challenges, researchers and practitioners can promote responsible and beneficial applications of machine learning technology.

3.3. DIAGNOSIS AND PROGNOSIS OF DISEASE

Machine learning techniques for disease diagnosis and prognosis have drawn a lot of attention recently because of their promise to increase diagnostic precision and effectiveness.

Diagnosis of Disease

Disease diagnosis using machine learning methods has become a promising field that could revolutionize healthcare. Machine learning, a subset of artificial intelligence, involves developing algorithms that can learn and make predictions or decisions based on patterns and data. To diagnose diseases, machine learning algorithms are trained using large amounts of medical data, including patient records, laboratory test results, medical imaging scans, genetic data and even text data from the scientific literature.

The main goal of using machine learning in disease diagnosis is to help healthcare professionals make accurate and timely diagnoses. By analyzing vast amounts of patient data, machine learning models can identify subtle patterns and relationships that may not be obvious to human observers. These models can then classify patients into different disease categories, predict the likelihood of certain diseases, or even identify specific disease subtypes.

However, applying machine learning to disease diagnosis involves several challenges. First, ensuring the quality and integrity of the input data is critical. Data bias or inaccuracies can lead to biased or unreliable forecasts. In addition, machine learning models must be validated and rigorously tested to assess their effectiveness and generalizability across different patient populations and healthcare settings.

In addition, the interpretability of machine learning models remains a concern in healthcare. Although these models can achieve impressive accuracy, understanding the reasons behind these predictions can be difficult. This lack of interpretability can raise ethical and legal issues, especially when patient care decisions are based solely on machine-generated results.

Disease	Precision	Recall	F1-score
Heart Disease	0.85	0.92	0.88
Diabetes	0.78	0.80	0.79
Lung Cancer	0.92	0.85	0.88
Parkinson's	0.93	0.96	0.94

In this table, accuracy is the percentage of properly detected instances among all expected positive cases, recall denotes the percentage among all actual positive cases, and F1-score combines precision and recall into a single metric.

Prognosis of Disease

Machine learning disease prediction involves the use of computer algorithms and statistical models to predict the likely course and outcome of a particular patient's disease. This field has received a lot of attention in recent years because it can help healthcare professionals make informed decisions, improve patient care, and optimize treatment strategies.

Machine learning techniques use large data sets consisting of patient data, medical data, laboratory results, genetic data and other relevant variables to develop predictive models. These models are trained to identify patterns and relationships in data and make predictions about future disease progression or outcomes. By analyzing massive amounts of data, machine learning algorithms can detect complex patterns that observers might miss. One of the main advantages of machine learning-based forecasting is its ability to provide personalized forecasts. Traditional prognostic methods are often based on population-level statistics and general guidelines that may not take into account the unique characteristics of each patient. On the other hand, machine learning models can take into account many individual factors such as age, gender, genetic markers, co-morbidities and treatment history. This personalized approach allows for more accurate and personalized prognoses for each patient.

Disease	Accuracy	Sensitivity	Specificity	AUC-ROC
Breast Cancer	0.87	0.80	0.92	0.89
Stroke	0.76	0.70	0.78	0.74
HIV/AIDS	0.92	0.88	0.94	0.93
Alzheimer's	0.81	0.75	0.84	0.80

In this table, accuracy denotes the proportion of overall correct predictions, sensitivity denotes the proportion of correctly identified true positive cases, specificity denotes the proportion of correctly identified true negative cases, and AUC-ROC (Area Under the Receiver Operating Characteristic curve) measures the model's overall performance.

3.4. MEDICAL IMAGING ANALYSIS

Machine learning algorithms are used to analyse and interpret medical pictures like X-rays, CT scans, MRI scans, and ultrasound images. This process is known as "medical imaging analysis." It entails the creation and application of algorithms and models that can automatically extract pertinent data from these images to support the diagnosis of diseases, the formulation of treatment plans, and the tracking of patient progress. By making it possible for more precise and effective analysis of medical pictures, this field has shown a lot of promise for enhancing healthcare results.

Here is an overview of the different techniques and their applications in medical imaging analysis:

Image Segmentation

Image segmentation is a fundamental task in the field of machine learning, which involves dividing an image into meaningful and distinguishable regions or objects. It plays a key role in computer vision applications such as object recognition, scene understanding, and autonomous driving.

The goal of image segmentation is to assign an identifier or class to each pixel in the image, effectively dividing the image into different regions based on their visual characteristics, such as color, texture, or shape. This process allows machines to identify and understand different objects or regions of an image, enabling more accurate analysis and decision making.

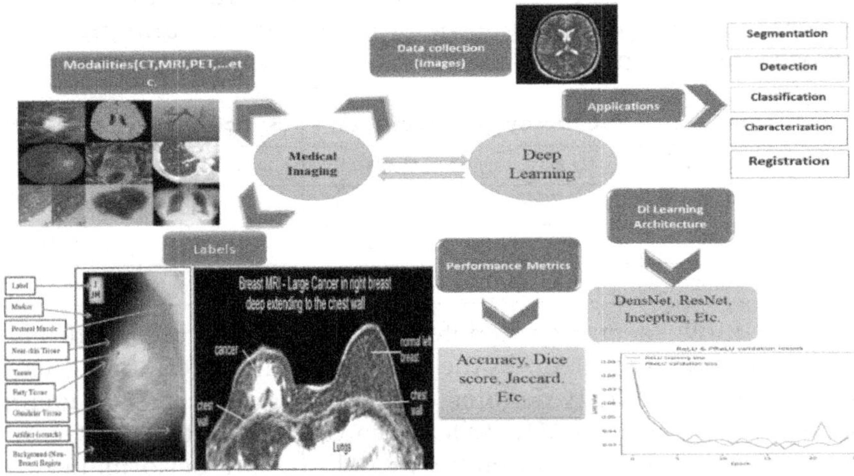

Medical Imaging Analysis

Several techniques and algorithms are used to segment images. Traditional methods include thresholding, region growing, and edge-based techniques based on predefined rules or heuristics that distinguish regions based on intensity or gradient information. However, these methods often struggle with complex or ambiguous images where features from different regions overlap.

3.5. DRUG DEVELOPMENT AND PERSONALIZED MEDICINE

Aiming to improve medication research and provide more individualised treatment plans, machine learning algorithms are used in this context to analyse vast amounts of biological data, identify trends, and make predictions.

Drug Development

Drug development is a complex and time-consuming process that involves the discovery, design, testing and approval of new drugs. Traditionally, this process has relied heavily on experimental approaches, which are often expensive, time-consuming, and often fail. However, in recent years, machine learning has become an effective tool to speed up and make the various stages of drug development more efficient.

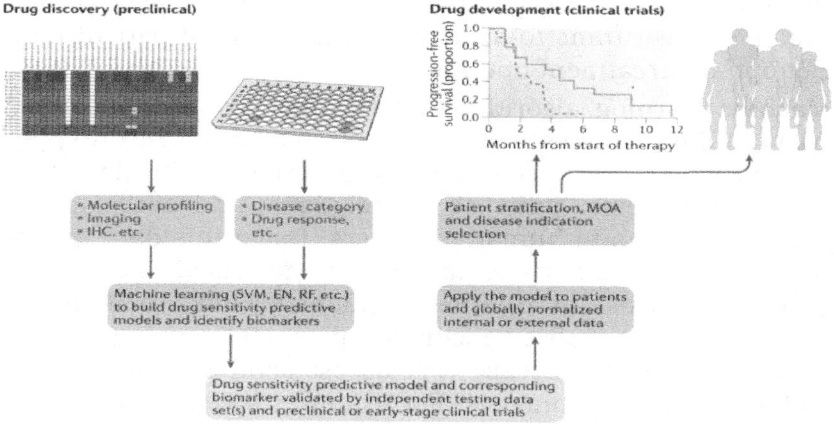

Drug Development

Machine learning algorithms can be used in the drug development process in many different ways. In the early stages of drug development, machine learning techniques can analyze big data such as genetic information, protein structures and chemical properties to identify potential drug targets and molecules with therapeutic potential. These algorithms can analyze patterns and relationships in data, helping researchers identify promising candidates more efficiently than traditional methods.

Another important application of machine learning in drug development is the prediction of drug toxicity and side effects. By analyzing vast databases of drug-related adverse events and patient data, machine learning algorithms can identify potential safety issues early in the development process, allowing researchers to make informed decisions about which compounds to favor and which to reject. In addition, machine learning can streamline the clinical trial process, a critical step in drug development. By analyzing patient data and real-world evidence, machine learning algorithms can help identify appropriate patient groups, optimize study design, and predict patient response. This can lead to more efficient and cost-effective clinical trials, ultimately accelerating the availability of new treatments to patients.

Personalized Medicine

Personalized medicine, also known as precision medicine, is an emerging field that aims to tailor treatment to individual patients based on their unique characteristics, including genetic makeup, lifestyle factors and environmental influences. Machine learning plays a critical role in advancing personalized medicine, using large data sets and complex algorithms to analyze vast amounts of patient data and predict optimal treatment options.

Machine learning algorithms can extract valuable insights from a variety of data sources, such as electronic health records, genome sequencing data, clinical trials, and real-time monitoring devices. These algorithms can detect patterns, correlations, and associations that may not be obvious to human observers. Using this data knowledge, healthcare professionals can make more informed decisions about diagnosis, prognosis and treatment options for individual patients. In the context of personalized medicine, machine learning models can be trained to develop disease risk assessment, treatment response, and adverse prediction models. For example, by analyzing a patient's genetic profile, lifestyle choices and medical history, machine learning algorithms can predict the likelihood of developing certain diseases, taking into account proactive and preventive measures.

3.6. REMOTE PATIENT MONITORING AND WEARABLE TECHNOLOGY

Wearable technology and remote patient monitoring (RPM) have grown in significance in the healthcare industry because they make it possible to continuously monitor patients' health outside of conventional healthcare settings. By offering individualised, real-time insights and early diagnosis of health concerns, these technologies have the potential to completely transform healthcare.

Remote Patient Monitoring (RPM)

Remote patient monitoring (RPM) is a medical practice that uses machine learning and other technological advances to monitor and collect patient health data outside of traditional healthcare settings. This approach allows healthcare providers to remotely monitor a patient's vital signs, symptoms and general well-being, enabling early detection of abnormalities or potential health risks.

Machine learning plays a key role in RPM as it processes and analyzes vast amounts of data collected from various tracking devices and sensors. Using advanced algorithms, machine learning models can identify patterns, identify trends and generate insights from collected data to help diagnose, treat and manage patients' diseases.

RPM uses wearable devices such as smart watches, fitness trackers and sensors that continuously monitor and record important vital signs such as heart rate, blood pressure, oxygen levels and activity levels. These devices transmit the collected data to a centralized system where machine learning algorithms can analyze the data in real time. Algorithms can compare patient data with historical data and established health standards, helping healthcare professionals identify anomalies or potential health risks.

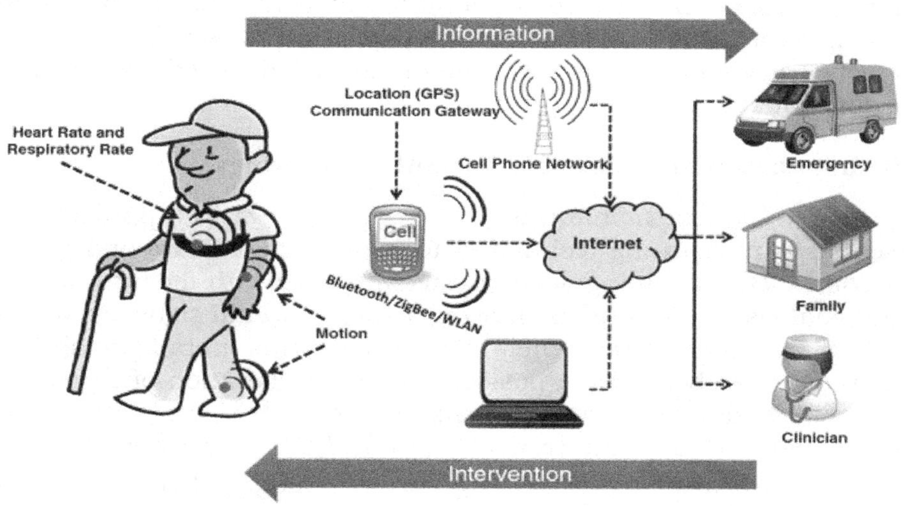

Remote Patient Monitoring and Wearable Technology

Table 1: Examples of Remote Patient Monitoring Data

Data Type	Examples
Vital Signs	Heart rate, blood pressure, respiratory rate
Activity Levels	Steps taken, calories burned, sleep patterns
Medication	Adherence to medication schedules
Glucose Levels	Continuous blood glucose monitoring

Wearable Technology

Wearable technology has advanced significantly in recent years, and its integration with machine learning has opened up new opportunities for innovation and applications. Machine learning algorithms are designed to analyze and interpret large volumes of data, and when combined with mobile devices, they can provide valuable insights and improve the user experience.

One area where wearable technology and machine learning intersect is in the field of health and fitness. Wearable devices such as smart watches, fitness trackers and biometric sensors collect information on various physiological parameters such as heart rate, sleep patterns and activity levels. Machine learning algorithms can process this data to identify patterns, identify anomalies, and provide personalized recommendations to improve health and wellness. Machine learning algorithms can, for example, analyze user activity data collected by a fitness tracker and provide insights to optimize exercise or detect signs of fatigue or overload. In addition, by continuously monitoring vital signs such as heart rate and sleep patterns, wearable devices can detect early warning signs of certain diseases and provide timely alerts or notifications.

Machine Learning in Remote Patient Monitoring

Remote patient monitoring (RPM) is an innovative approach that uses machine learning techniques to improve healthcare and patient outcomes. By combining advanced technologies with medical devices, RPM enables continuous monitoring of patients' vital signs, symptoms and health status from their own home. This paradigm shift in healthcare has been made possible by the proliferation of Internet of Things (IoT) devices, wearable sensors and mobile applications that collect real-time data and transmit it to healthcare providers.

Machine learning plays a key role in remote patient monitoring as it processes and analyzes the vast amount of data produced by these monitoring devices. With advanced algorithms, machine learning algorithms can identify patterns, correlations and anomalies in data, allowing healthcare professionals to make more accurate diagnoses, detect early signs of deterioration and customize treatment plans. One of the main applications of machine learning in remote patient monitoring is predictive analytics. By training models on historical patient data, machine learning algorithms can predict potential health problems and predict the likelihood of hospital readmissions or adverse events. This allows healthcare providers to intervene proactively, provide timely interventions and reduce the risk of complications.

3.7. VIRTUAL ASSISTANTS AND TELEMEDICINE

Virtual Assistants and Telemedicine in Machine Learning

Machine learning has a major impact on the way healthcare is delivered in two areas, virtual assistants and telemedicine. Virtual assistants can comprehend customer inquiries and provide answers thanks to machine learning algorithms, which can aid medical experts in providing precise diagnoses. On the other side, telemedicine uses machine learning to provide personalised therapy recommendations and remote patient monitoring.

Virtual Assistants

Machine learning virtual assistants refer to intelligent computer programs or applications that use machine learning techniques to provide automated support and assistance to users. These virtual assistants are designed to understand natural language commands or questions and respond with relevant information or perform specific tasks.

Machine learning plays a crucial role in virtual assistants, as they can learn from user interactions and improve their performance over time. These assistants use technologies such as natural language processing (NLP), speech recognition and sentiment analysis to accurately understand and interpret user input. They can extract meaning from text or voice commands, identify user intent and generate relevant responses. One of the main advantages of virtual assistants powered by machine learning is their ability to adapt and adapt their responses based on individual user preferences. By analyzing user behavior, patterns and historical data, these assistants can learn to anticipate user needs, make personalized recommendations and deliver a personalized user experience.

Telemedicine

Telemedicine, a field that combines telecommunications and medicine, has made significant progress with the integration of machine learning techniques. Machine learning is a subset of artificial intelligence (AI) that allows computer systems to learn from data and analyze it, make predictions and make decisions without special programming. In the context of telemedicine, machine learning algorithms are used to analyze large amounts of medical data, extract valuable insights and diagnose diseases, monitor patient health and optimize treatment plans.

One of the most important applications of machine learning in telemedicine is medical image analysis. Radiology and pathology are fields where machine learning algorithms excel at pattern recognition, detecting abnormalities and making accurate diagnoses. These algorithms can be trained on large data sets of medical images, allowing them to learn to recognize certain features and predict possible diseases or conditions. For example, deep learning algorithms have shown remarkable effectiveness in detecting tumors in medical scans such as X-rays, MRIs and CT scans, helping radiologists make early detection and provide more accurate diagnoses.

Application	Description	Machine Learning Applications
Remote Monitoring	Collecting and analyzing patient data remotely	Predictive analytics for early detection of deteriorating health conditions
Image Analysis	Analyzing medical images for diagnosis and treatment planning	Computer-aided diagnosis, tumor detection, and radiology image analysis
Electronic Health Records (EHR)	Efficient management and analysis of patient health records	Natural language processing for EHR data extraction and clinical decision support
Personalized Treatment	Tailoring treatment plans based on patient-specific data	Predictive modeling for personalized medicine and treatment recommendations

Deep learning neural networks and other machine learning algorithms help create precise virtual assistants and make it possible for telemedicine systems to deliver effective, individualised treatment. These innovations could increase patient outcomes, facilitate clinical workflows, and increase access to healthcare.

Integration into Clinical Workflow

Integrating into the clinical workflow means incorporating machine learning techniques and processes into the existing healthcare framework. It involves the seamless integration of advanced algorithms and data-driven models with traditional clinical practices to improve patient care, diagnostic accuracy and overall health outcomes.

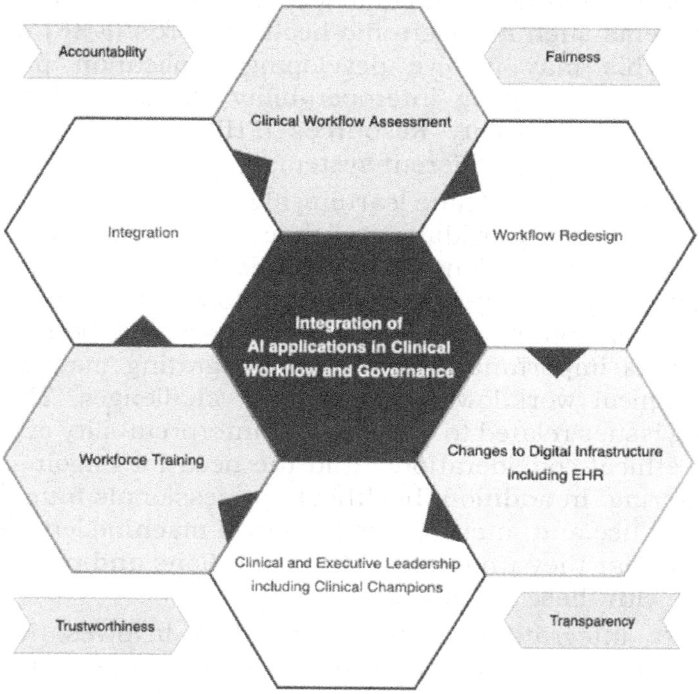

Integration into Clinical Workflow

Integrating machine learning into the clinical workflow requires several key steps. First, it is necessary to identify specific areas where machine learning can add value, such as image analysis, predictive analysis or risk stratification. Once these areas are identified, relevant data sets must be collected, including electronic health records, medical imaging data, genomic data and other relevant sources. Data processing and standardization are crucial to ensure quality and consistency of input data. This includes cleaning the data, removing outliers, handling missing values, and normalizing variables. In addition, privacy and data security measures must be implemented to protect patient confidentiality and comply with regulations such as the Health Insurance Portability and Accountability Act (HIPAA).

Once the data is ready, machine learning algorithms can be trained using supervised, unsupervised or reinforcement learning techniques, depending on the task at hand. Model development and evaluation are iterative processes that involve fine-tuning algorithms, confirming their performance on independent data sets, and evaluating their generalizability. Integration into clinical workflow requires collaboration between data scientists, clinicians and other healthcare stakeholders. Machine learning models must be embedded in existing clinical systems such as electronic health records (EHR) or radiology platforms. This may involve developing application programming interfaces (APIs) or using interoperability standards such as Fast Healthcare Interoperability Resources (FHIR) to facilitate seamless data exchange between different systems.

When integrated, machine learning algorithms can support clinical decision-making by providing real-time predictions, risk scores or treatment recommendations. For example, they can help with early disease detection, identify high-risk patients who may need preventive intervention, or optimize treatment plans based on personal factors. However, it is important to note that integrating machine learning into the clinical workflow is not without challenges. This requires addressing issues related to data quality, interpretability of algorithms, legal and ethical considerations, and the need for ongoing validation and monitoring. In addition, healthcare professionals must be trained to effectively use and interpret the results of machine learning models and ensure that they understand the limitations and potential biases associated with these technologies.

In short, integration in clinical workflow involves the seamless integration of machine learning into healthcare systems to improve clinical decision-making, improve patient outcomes and improve overall healthcare performance. This requires careful consideration of data, algorithm development, collaboration between stakeholders, and continuous monitoring to ensure safe and effective use of machine learning in clinical settings.

3.8. FUTURE PLANS FOR HEALTHCARE MACHINE LEARNING

Machine learning has the ability to completely transform many facets of patient care, diagnosis, treatment, and research in the healthcare industry.

1. Disease Diagnosis and Prognosis: Machine learning disease diagnosis and prognosis refers to the application of computer algorithms and techniques to analyze medical data and make accurate predictions about diseases and their future outcomes. This field combines the skills of machine learning, data mining, and statistical analysis to help healthcare professionals make informed decisions and improve patient care.

Machine learning algorithms are trained to use vast amounts of medical data such as patient records, medical imaging scans, lab test results and genetic information to diagnose diseases. These algorithms learn patterns and relationships in the data to accurately identify and classify diseases. By analyzing a patient's symptoms and medical history, machine learning models can help detect diseases such as cancer, cardiovascular disease, infectious diseases and neurological diseases early. In addition, machine learning plays a key role in disease prognosis, which involves predicting disease progression and potential outcomes. By analyzing historical patient data, treatment responses, and other important factors, machine learning models can generate predictive information that helps with treatment, disease management, and patient counseling. These models can estimate the likelihood of disease progression, recurrence, survival and potential complications, allowing healthcare providers to adjust treatment strategies and optimize patient outcomes.

Machine learning methods used in disease diagnosis and prognosis include classification algorithms (such as decision trees, support vector machines and random forests), regression models, deep learning neural networks and ensemble methods. These algorithms can process complex and high-dimensional data, extract meaningful features, and discover hidden patterns that may not be visible to human observers. Although machine learning algorithms have shown promise in disease diagnosis and prognosis, it is important to note that they should be used as complementary tools, not substitutes for clinical knowledge. Health professionals remain an integral part of the decision-making process. They interpret and confirm algorithm predictions, consider individual patient factors and provide personalized care.

Overall, machine learning disease diagnosis and prognosis offers great potential to revolutionize healthcare, enabling earlier and more accurate diagnoses, individualized treatment plans and better patient outcomes. Continued research and collaboration between machine learning experts and medical professionals are critical to advancing the field and realizing its full potential in clinical practice.

Application	**Description**
Image-based Diagnosis	Using deep learning models to analyze medical images for diagnosis.
Risk Prediction Models	Developing algorithms to predict the risk of developing diseases.
Precision Medicine	Identifying patient-specific treatment options based on genetics.

2. Electronic Health Records (EHRs) and Patient Data Analysis: Electronic health records (EHR) have revolutionized the healthcare industry by digitizing patient health information and enabling efficient storage, retrieval and analysis. EHR records contain comprehensive patient information, including medical history, diagnoses, medications, lab results, and treatment plans. This large amount of data provides a valuable opportunity for machine learning and data analysis techniques to gain meaningful insights and improve patient care.

Machine learning algorithms can be applied to EHR systems to identify patterns and trends that may not be immediately apparent to healthcare providers. By analyzing large data sets, these algorithms can uncover hidden correlations, predict disease progression, and identify risk factors for certain diseases. For example, machine learning models can be trained to predict a heart failure patient's likelihood of being readmitted based on their EHR data, allowing healthcare providers to proactively intervene and reduce hospitalizations.

In addition, machine learning can play a crucial role in precision medicine by tailoring treatment to individual patients. By analyzing EHRs, machine learning algorithms can identify subgroups of patients who are more likely to respond positively to a particular treatment or who are at greater risk of side effects. Such an individual approach can significantly improve treatment results and reduce the occurrence of side effects.

Another application of machine learning in EHR analytics is the detection of outliers or outliers in patient data. By comparing a patient's data with a large number of similar cases, algorithms can flag unusual patterns that could indicate potential health problems or errors in the data. This can help healthcare providers identify and correct anomalies in patient data and ensure data accuracy.

However, it is important to address the challenges associated with EHR and patient data analytics. Privacy and data security are paramount because EHRs contain sensitive patient information. Healthcare organizations must adhere to strict regulations and implement strong security measures to protect patient confidentiality and prevent data breaches. In addition, the quality and completeness of EHR data can vary, which can affect the accuracy and reliability of machine learning models. Data cleaning and pre-processing techniques are critical to ensure that input data is consistent and error-free.

In conclusion, the combination of EHR and machine learning has tremendous potential to improve health outcomes. Using the vast amount of patient data in EHRs, machine learning algorithms can provide valuable insights, enable personalized medicine, detect anomalies, and support evidence-based decision-making. However, it is important to address privacy concerns and ensure data quality to maximize the benefits of EHR-based analytics in healthcare.

Application	Description
Predictive Analytics	Using historical patient data to predict outcomes and risks.
Anomaly Detection	Identifying unusual patterns or outliers in patient data.
Real-time Monitoring	Monitoring patients continuously and alerting for critical events.

3. Drug Discovery and Development: Drug discovery and development is a complex and time-consuming process that involves the identification, design and optimization of potential therapeutic compounds for the treatment of diseases. In recent years, machine learning has become a promising tool in this field, revolutionizing the way new drugs are discovered and developed.

Machine learning techniques use large data sets, including molecular structures, genetic data, clinical data and biological analyses, to reveal patterns, relationships and insights that can aid the drug development process. One of the main applications of machine learning in this field is virtual screening, in which algorithms analyze huge libraries of compounds to identify those most likely to bind to a specific target, such as a disease-related protein.

These algorithms can significantly accelerate the early stages of drug development by reducing the pool of potential compounds for further investigation. By predicting the binding affinity of a compound to a target, machine learning models can prioritize the most promising candidates, reducing the need for time-consuming and expensive experimental testing.

In addition, machine learning plays a key role in the optimization and design of drug candidates. Algorithms can generate and evaluate thousands or even millions of virtual compounds, optimizing their properties based on desired criteria such as potency, selectivity and safety. This computational approach helps identify compounds with a higher chance of success, guiding the decision-making process before expensive and time-consuming experimental validation begins.

Machine learning also helps predict the pharmacokinetic and toxicological properties of potential drug candidates. These models can analyze molecular properties and historical data to estimate the behavior of a compound in the human body, including absorption, distribution, metabolism and excretion. By identifying potential risks and liabilities early, researchers can focus their efforts on compounds with better chances of success and better safety profiles.

Application	Description
Virtual Screening	Predicting the interaction between drug molecules and targets.
De Novo Drug Design	Generating new drug compounds with desired properties.
Drug Repurposing	Identifying existing drugs for new therapeutic uses.

4. Personalized Treatment and Care: Personalized care and care in machine learning refers to the application of advanced computing technologies to tailor health interventions and services to individual patients according to their unique characteristics and needs. This approach uses the ability of machine learning algorithms to analyze large amounts of data, including patient data, genetic information, lifestyle factors and treatment outcomes, to generate insights and predictions that can guide personalized health decisions.

By integrating machine learning into the health sector, personalized care and treatment aims to move away from a one-size-fits-all approach and provide targeted interventions that are more effective, efficient and patient-friendly. These algorithms can identify patterns, correlations, and risk factors that may not be immediately obvious to healthcare providers. By analyzing vast amounts of data, machine learning models can reveal hidden relationships, predict disease, identify optimal treatment strategies and even detect subtle changes that may indicate the need for early intervention. One major advantage of individual treatment is the possibility to optimize treatment plans and reduce side effects. Machine learning models can be used to assess patient characteristics such as genetic predispositions, co-morbidities and medical history, and determine the most appropriate treatment methods and dosage. This personalized approach can improve treatment results and minimize the risk of side effects or ineffectiveness.

In conclusion, personalized care and care in machine learning offer enormous potential to revolutionize healthcare by tailoring interventions to individual patients. By harnessing the power of data and algorithms, healthcare providers can optimize their care plans, improve patient outcomes, and improve the overall quality and efficiency of healthcare. However, the responsible development and deployment of these technologies are critical for ethical considerations and to ensure patient privacy and well-being.

Application	Description
Genomic Medicine	Analyzing genetic data to personalize treatment strategies.
Treatment Recommendations	Recommending treatment options based on patient characteristics.
Continuous Monitoring	Using wearable devices to monitor patients and provide feedback.

5. Healthcare Operations and Resource Management: Healthcare operations and resource management in machine learning refers to the application of artificial intelligence and data analytics techniques to optimize various aspects of healthcare. It uses machine learning algorithms to analyze vast amounts of health data and make informed decisions about the allocation and use of health system resources.

One of the main areas where machine learning can be useful is predicting patient demand and resource utilization. By analyzing historical patient data, machine learning models can predict future patient volumes, allowing healthcare providers to allocate resources efficiently. This includes predicting patient appointments, emergency room visits and the need for special medical procedures. With accurate forecasts, hospitals and clinics can better plan staffing levels, manage bed capacity and allocate resources such as medical equipment and supplies.

Another important part of healthcare operations and resource management is optimizing program and appointment booking systems. Machine learning algorithms can analyze patient preferences, historical appointment data and other relevant factors to create optimized software solutions. This helps reduce patient wait times, increase healthcare provider utilization and improve overall operational efficiency.

Machine learning also plays a key role in optimizing inventory management in healthcare environments. By analyzing historical drug and medical supply usage data, machine learning models can predict future demand, identify patterns and optimize inventory levels accordingly. This ensures that healthcare facilities have sufficient supplies while minimizing waste and reducing costs.

Application	Description
Demand Forecasting	Predicting patient admission rates and resource requirements.
Staff Scheduling	Optimizing healthcare staff schedules based on demand.
Fraud Detection	Identifying fraudulent activities in healthcare insurance claims.

These instances highlight the various ways that machine learning is used in healthcare. Further developments in algorithms, data accessibility, and processing capacity are anticipated to uncover even greater possibilities for machine learning in enhancing patient care, research, and healthcare operations. The area is constantly evolving.

4

Machine Learning in Finance: Revolutionizing the Future of Financial Analysis

4.1. INTRODUCTION TO MACHINE LEARNING IN FINANCE

Overview of Machine Learning

Machine learning is a branch of artificial intelligence (AI) that focuses on developing algorithms and models that can learn from data and make predictions or decisions without special programming. It involves the use of statistical techniques and computing power to enable computers to analyse and interpret complex patterns and relationships in large data sets. By learning from historical data, machine learning algorithms can generalize and make accurate predictions or take appropriate actions when they encounter new, unseen data.

Development and Applications in Various Industries

Machine learning has advanced significantly in recent years due to the availability of large datasets, increased computing power and algorithmic innovations. These developments have allowed machine learning to find applications in a variety of industries, including healthcare, retail, manufacturing and finance.

In healthcare, machine learning algorithms can analyse patient data to aid in diagnosis, predict disease outcomes, and customize treatment plans. In retail, machine learning is used for demand forecasting, customer segmentation and recommendation systems. In manufacturing, machine learning techniques are applied to optimize production processes, identify anomalies and predict maintenance needs. In the financial sector, machine learning has transformed various aspects of finance, from asset management and trading to risk assessment and fraud detection. The ability to analyse large financial data, including historical market data, financial indicators, news sentiment and transaction data, enables financial institutions to make informed decisions and automate complex tasks.

The Importance of Machine Learning in the Economy

Machine learning plays a key role in finance due to the huge amount of data and the need for fast and accurate decision making. Financial institutions deal with stock prices, interest rates, credit ratings, market trends and countless other factors that affect investment strategies, risk assessment and profitability.

By leveraging machine learning in finance, companies can harness the power of advanced analytics and predictive models to gain a competitive advantage. Machine learning algorithms can identify complex patterns and relationships in financial data that may not be obvious to human analysts. These algorithms can make accurate forecasts, assess risks, optimize portfolios and automate trading strategies.

Main Challenges of Economic Analysis

Traditional financial analysis methods often struggle to deal with the complexity and volume of financial data. Financial data is characterized by its high dimension, noise, missing values and non-linearity. Traditional statistical models may not adequately describe the underlying patterns and relationships in the data, leadi n g to suboptimal predictions and decisions.

Financial analysis also involves handling time dependencies and incorporating unstructured data sources such as news articles, social media sentiment and economic indicators. Traditional methods may not be able to effectively capture the time-varying nature of financial information and may not incorporate qualitative information from unstructured sources. In addition, economic analysis often requires dealing with unbalanced data sets, where positive and negative cases are not equally distributed. For example, when assessing credit risk, the number of defaults is usually much lower than the number of non-defaults. Traditional models may struggle to accurately predict minority class performances and may be biased towards the majority class.

Potential Benefits of Machine Learning to Overcome Challenges

Machine learning techniques offer a number of advantages in addressing the challenges of financial analysis. Accurate predictions:

machine learning algorithms can analyse historical data and pick up complex patterns and trends may affect future results. By training on large amounts of data, these algorithms can make accurate predictions, such as the movement of share prices, the probability of credit risk default, or the probability of loan repayment. Risk assessment and management: Machine learning algorithms can assess risk by analysing historical data and identifying patterns that indicate potential risks. For example, credit risk models can predict the probability of default based on historical credit data. By accurately assessing risk, financial institutions can make informed decisions about lending, investment strategies and risk mitigation.

- **Automation and efficiency:** Machine learning can automate labour-intensive financial management tasks such as data processing, portfolio optimization and trade execution. This automation reduces manual errors, saves time and allows analysts to focus on more valuable tasks. Fraud detection: machine learning algorithms can identify patterns and anomalies in financial transactions to detect fraud. By analysing historical event data and identifying unusual patterns, machine learning algorithms can flag suspicious events for further investigation.
- **Personalized financial services:** Machine learning techniques can analyse customer data and behaviour to provide personalized financial services and recommendations. This includes individual investment strategies, loan proposals and insurance plans tailored to individual needs and risk profiles.

4.2. PORTFOLIO OPTIMIZATION AND STOCK MARKET PREDICTION

Portfolio Optimization

In the financial sector, portfolio optimization is a key task in creating an investment portfolio that maximizes returns and minimizes risk. The goal is to find an optimal asset allocation that strikes a balance between the desired level of return and the acceptable level of risk. Machine learning techniques have become powerful tools to improve portfolio optimization by capturing complex relationships between assets and incorporating dynamic market conditions.

Traditional Mean-variance Optimization

One of the widely used portfolio optimization approaches is Mean-Variance Optimization (MVO), which is based on the Modern Portfolio

Theory (MPT) developed by Harry Markowitz. The objective of MVO is to find an asset allocation that ensures the highest expected return at a given risk level. It takes into account the expected return; the covariance matrix of asset returns and the risk tolerance of the investor.

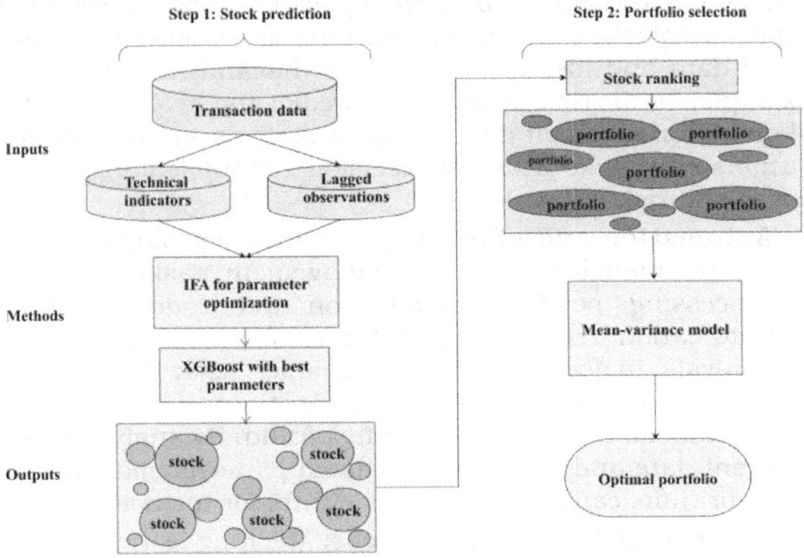

In MVO, an efficient frontier is constructed to represent the set of portfolios that offer the highest expected return for each level of risk. The optimal portfolio is on the efficient frontier based on the risk habits of the investor. The optimization problem can be solved using mathematical programming techniques such as quadratic programming.

Machine Learning in Portfolio Optimization

Machine learning techniques offer innovative solutions to improve portfolio optimization by capturing complex patterns and interactions between assets. These techniques can handle non-linear relationships, add additional factors and adapt to dynamic market conditions.

Forecasting Models

Machine learning models, such as regression models or time series forecasting models, can be trained on historical data to predict asset returns or risk measures. These predictions can then be used as input to the paper optimization process. By incorporating predictive models, the portfolio construction process becomes more data-driven and able to capture non-linear dependencies between assets.

Reinforcement of Learning

Reinforcement learning is another approach that can be used in portfolio optimization. It treats portfolio management as a sequential decision problem and formulates it as a Markov decision process (MDP). The agent learns to make asset allocation and balancing decisions through trial and error in a dynamic environment. By interacting with the market and receiving rewards or punishments based on portfolio performance, the agent learns optimal principles for portfolio management.

Factor-based Models

Factor-based models use machine learning techniques to identify and incorporate additional factors that affect asset returns. These factors can be financial indicators, company-specific financial indicators, or even opinion polls from news and social media. By considering these factors, the model can better describe the risk and return dynamics of different assets and build stronger portfolios.

Advanced Technologies and Limitations

Machine learning techniques make it possible to add additional constraints and considerations to portfolio optimization.

Transaction Costs and Liquidity Limits

Machine learning algorithms can handle complex optimization problems that take into account transaction costs and liquidity constraints. These limitations are crucial in real-world portfolio management because they affect the feasibility and profitability of trading strategies. By integrating these constraints into the optimization process, machine learning algorithms can create portfolios that are more practical and consistent with the investor's goals.

Custom Goals

With the help of machine learning, investors can adjust their goals in addition to traditional risk-reward relationships. For example, an investor may want to maximize the Sharpe ratio (a measure of risk-adjusted return) or achieve a certain level of protection against impairment. Machine learning algorithms can optimize portfolios based on these customized goals and provide customized solutions that suit specific investment preferences.

Visualization of Portfolio Optimization

Visualization plays a crucial role in understanding and interpreting the results of portfolio optimization. They provide an overview of the relationship between risk and return, the composition of optimal portfolios and the impact of various constraints or factors.

The efficient frontier is a commonly used visualization to describe the relationship between risk and return. It shows the set of portfolios that offer the highest expected return for each level of risk. Portfolios on the efficient frontier are considered optimal based on the risk preferences of the investor.

Another visualization technique involves presenting the optimal portfolio. It shows the allocation percentages of different assets in the portfolio, giving a clear view of the diversification strategy.

Visualizing a portfolio's historical performance can also help assess its risk and return characteristics. A line chart or candlestick charts can be used to represent the cumulative performance of a portfolio over time, allowing investors to analyse trends and make informed decisions.

In summary, machine learning techniques offer significant improvements in portfolio optimization in finance. By incorporating predictive models, reinforcement learning, factor-based models and constraints, machine learning algorithms can create portfolios that are better able to capture complex relationships, adapt to dynamic market conditions and meet specific investment objectives. Visualizations help you understand results even better and make informed investment decisions.

Stock Market Prediction

Stock market forecasting is a difficult task to predict future prices and trends in financial markets. Machine learning techniques have gained considerable popularity in the industry due to their ability to analyse vast amounts of historical data and identify patterns that can help make predictions.

Data Pre-processing and Operational Planning

Before using machine learning algorithms to predict the stock market, it is important to pre-process and shape the data. This includes operations such as cleaning the data, handling missing values and converting the data into a format suitable for analysis.

In addition, feature design plays an important role in extracting relevant information from the data. Real estate prices can be derived from a variety of sources, including price data, volume data, technical indicators, and macroeconomic factors. For example, common technical indicators such as moving averages, Relative Strength Index (RSI) and Bollinger Bands can provide valuable information about market trends and momentum.

Supervised Learning for Stock Market Forecasting

Supervised learning algorithms can be used to predict future stock prices based on historical data and meaningful characteristics. Regression models such as linear regression or support vector regression (SVR) are commonly used for this task.

The training data is divided into an input variable (X) and a target variable (Y), which represents the future stock prices. The model learns the relationship between the features and the target variable and can then make predictions based on unseen data.

Time Series Analysis for Stock Market Forecasting

There are temporal dependencies in stock market data, where the order of observations is important. Time series analysis techniques such as ARIMA (Autoregressive Integrated Moving Average) models or Long Short-Term Memory (LSTM) networks can be used to forecast stock markets.

ARIMA models capture the autoregressive (AR), moving average (MA), and variance (I) components of time series data. These models can capture seasonality, trends, and other time-dependent patterns in the data. On the other hand, LSTM networks are recurrent neural networks (RNNs) that can learn long-term dependencies from sequential data. They are particularly effective at capturing complex patterns and trends in stock market data.

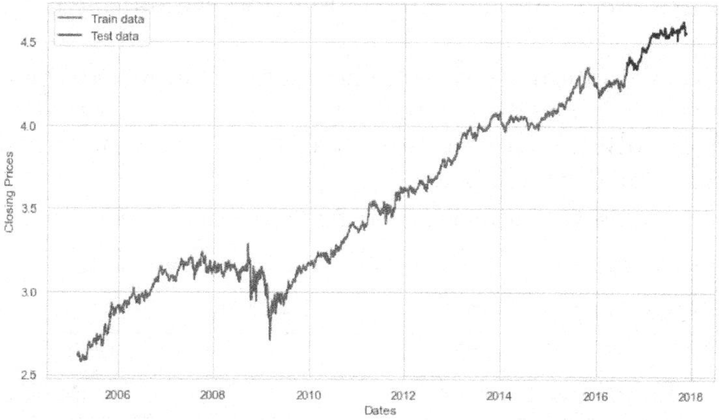

In figure 1, we introduce the use of time series analysis techniques in stock market forecasting. The model learns from historical stock price data and gathers patterns and trends to make future price predictions.

Ensemble Learning for Stock Market Forecasting

Ensemble learning techniques can be useful for forecasting stock markets by combining the forecasts of several individual models. Bagging, boosting, and random forests are popular machine learning techniques that can improve prediction accuracy and robustness.

Random forests combine multiple decision trees, each trained to make predictions based on a random subset of the data. All this reduces the risk of overfitting and improves the generalizability of the model.

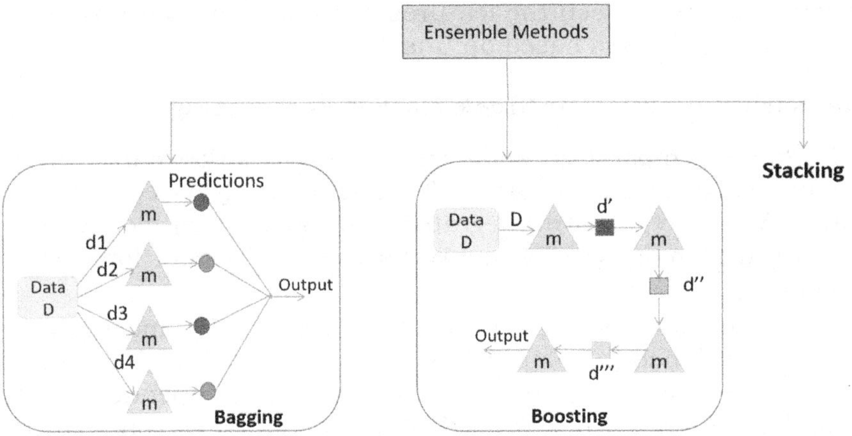

In Figure 2, illustrates the concept of aggregate learning for stock market forecasting. Several individual models, such as decision trees, are combined into a random forest that together makes predictions about future stock prices. 5.6 Metrics for evaluating stock market forecasts

Various evaluation metrics can be used to evaluate the performance of stock market forecasting models. Commonly used metrics are mean square error (MSE), mean absolute error (MAE), root mean square error (RMSE), and heading accuracy.

Table 1: Evaluation Metrics for Stock Market Prediction

Metric	Formula
Mean Squared Error	MSE = (1/N) ∑(Y_true - Y_pred)^2
Mean Absolute Error	MAE = (1/N) ∑
Root Mean Squared Error	RMSE = sqrt(MSE)

Table 1 provides an overview of valuation metrics used in stock market forecasting. These metrics help evaluate the accuracy and performance of models in predicting future stock prices.

In summary, stock market forecasting using machine learning techniques involves data processing, feature design, and application of various algorithms such as supervised learning, time series analysis, and ensemble learning. Evaluation metrics provide insight into the performance of these models. Using these techniques, investors and financial institutions can make more informed decisions and improve their trading strategies in the dynamic and complex world of the stock market.

4.3. ANTI-MONEY LAUNDERING (AML) AND FRAUD DETECTION

Anti-money laundering (AML) and fraud detection are important tasks in the financial industry. Money laundering involves concealing the origin of illegally obtained funds and making them legal. Fraud, on the other hand, refers to misleading actions that cause financial loss to individuals, organizations or the entire financial system. Machine learning techniques have become increasingly important in AML and fraud detection due to their ability to analyse large amounts of financial data and identify patterns and anomalies that may indicate suspicious activity.

Data Pre-processing and Function Design

Data pre-processing is a key step in AML and fraud detection. This involves cleaning and modifying raw data to ensure its quality and usability. This may include handling missing values, removing outliers, and normalizing or scaling the data.

Feature planning is another important part of the data processing step. This includes creating new features or selecting relevant features from available data that can provide valuable information for fraud detection. These characteristics can be derived from a variety of sources, including transactional data, customer data, geographic data, and historical behavioural patterns. For example, characteristics such as transaction volume, transaction frequency, transaction time and geographic location can be useful in identifying potential money laundering or fraud.

Table 1 shows an example of the structure of the AML and fraud detection functions. In addition to the basic transaction information such as transaction ID, amount, source account, destination account, transaction type and timestamp, there is an additional feature called

"Distance", which represents the geographical distance between the source and destination. This additional feature can help detect fraudulent activity involving transactions in remote locations.

Table 1: Example of Feature Engineering for AML and Fraud Detection

Transaction ID	Amount ($)	Source Account	Destination Account	Transaction Type	Time Stamp	Distance (km)
1	1000	A1	B1	Transfer	2020-01-01 09:30:00	10.2
2	5000	C1	B2	Deposit	2020-01-01 10:15:00	5.6
3	2000	D1	B1	Transfer	2020-01-01 11:20:00	15.1

Guided Learning of AML and Fraud Detection

Supervised learning algorithms can be used to detect AML and fraud when labelled data is available, classifying each transaction as either legitimate or fraudulent. Classification algorithms such as logistic regression, decision trees, random forests and support vector machines (SVM) are often used for this purpose. Labelled training data is used to train a machine learning model to identify patterns and characteristics of fraudulent transactions. The model can then make predictions based on new, unlabelled data to detect potential fraud.

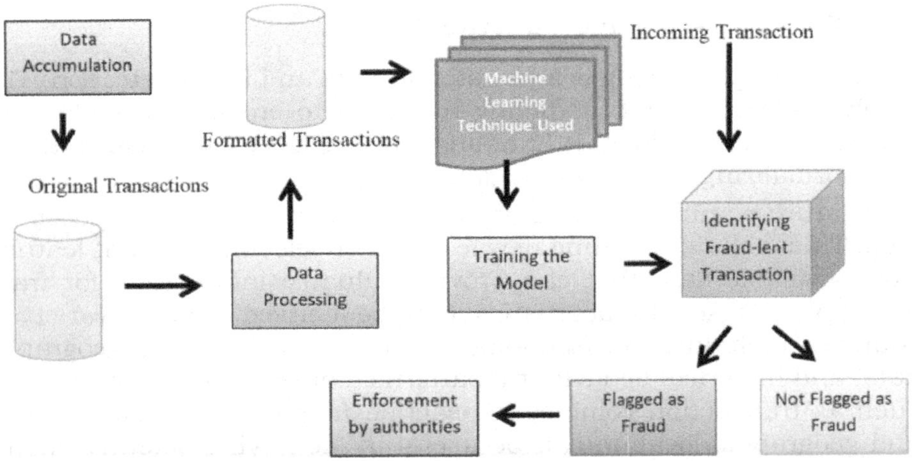

Figure 1 illustrates AML and fraud detection monitoring. The model learns from historical transaction data with known identifiers and uses this information to predict whether new transactions are legitimate or fraudulent.

Unsupervised AML and Fraud Detection

Unsupervised learning methods are useful when there is little or no labelled data, because they can automatically detect patterns and anomalies in data. Anomaly detection algorithms, clustering algorithms, and density-based approaches are commonly used unsupervised learning methods for AML and fraud detection.

Clustering algorithms group similar events together based on their characteristics, which allows for the identification of clusters that deviate from the behaviour of the majority. This can help identify potential fraud clusters or money laundering networks. Density-based approaches such as Isolation Forest and Local Outlier Factor detect outliers based on the density of data points. They detect events in sparser areas of information dissemination, indicating potentially fraudulent activity.

AML and Fraud Detection Network Analysis

Network analysis techniques are valuable in detecting complex fraud and money laundering operations involving multiple interconnected parties. By analysing relationships and transactions between accounts, graph-based algorithms can uncover hidden relationships and detect suspicious patterns.

Network analysis involves creating a graphical representation of a financial system, where nodes represent accounts and edges represent transactions between them. Different algorithms such as centrality measures, community detection and path analysis can be applied to identify key players, suspicious clusters and online money flows.

Table 2: Example of Network Analysis for AML and Fraud Detection

Source Account	Destination Account	Transaction Count
A1	B1	100
B1	C1	50
C1	D1	75

Table 2 shows an example of network analysis for AML and fraud detection. It shows the transaction volume between source and target accounts, which can help identify accounts involved in suspicious activity based on unusually high transaction volumes or circular transactions.

AML and Fraud Detection Evaluation Metrics

Different evaluation metrics can be used to evaluate the performance of AML and fraud detection models, depending on the specific requirements and characteristics of the problem. Commonly used metrics are precision, accuracy, recall, F1 score and area under the receiver operating curve (AUC-ROC).

Accuracy measures the overall accuracy of the model's predictions, while accuracy indicates the proportion of correctly detected fraudulent transactions out of all predicted fraud cases. Recall, also known as sensitivity or true positive rate, measures the proportion of correctly detected fraudulent transactions out of all true fraud cases. The F1 score is a harmonic mean of precision and recall, providing a balanced measure of model performance. AUC-ROC represents the model's ability to distinguish between fraudulent and legitimate transactions, with a higher value indicating better performance.

Table 3: Evaluation Metrics for AML and Fraud Detection

Metric	Formula
Accuracy	(True Positives + True Negatives) / Total Transactions
Precision	True Positives / (True Positives + False Positives)
Recall	True Positives / (True Positives + False Negatives)
F1-score	2 * (Precision * Recall) / (Precision + Recall)
AUC-ROC	Area under the ROC curve

Table 3 summarizes the AML and fraud detection evaluation metric used. These metrics provide valuable information about the functionality of the models and help financial institutions evaluate their effectiveness in detecting and preventing fraud.

In summary, AML and fraud detection use machine learning techniques such as data pre-processing, feature engineering, supervised and unsupervised learning, and network analysis. These techniques can be used to analyse large amounts of financial data, identify patterns and detect anomalies that may indicate suspicious activity. Using these methods and assessment metrics, financial institutions can improve their ability to combat money laundering and fraud and ensure the integrity and security of the financial system.

4.4. LOAN APPROVAL AND CREDIT RISK ASSESSMENT

Loan approval and credit risk assessment are key processes in the banking and finance industry. When individuals or companies apply for a loan, financial institutions must assess their creditworthiness and likelihood of repaying the loan. Traditionally, these assessments were done manually, which was time-consuming and prone to human error. But with machine learning, automated algorithms can analyse vast amounts of data and provide accurate risk assessments.

Data Pre-processing and Operational Planning

Data pre-processing is an important step in loan approval and credit risk assessment. This involves cleaning and modifying raw data to ensure its quality and consistency. This may include handling missing values, handling outliers, and normalizing or scaling the data to make it suitable for analysis.

Feature planning is another important part of the data processing step. This includes creating new features or selecting relevant features from existing data that can contribute to accurate risk analysis. For example, characteristics such as income, employment status, credit history, loan amount, loan term and debt-to-income ratio can provide valuable information about an applicant's creditworthiness.

Table 1: Example of Feature Engineering for Credit Risk Assessment

Customer ID	Age	Income ($)	Employment Status	Loan Amount ($)	Loan Term (months)	Credit Score
1	30	50000	Employed	10000	24	750
2	45	80000	Self-employed	25000	36	680
3	28	35000	Unemployed	5000	12	600

Table 1 shows an example of credit risk assessment. In addition to basic customer information, features such as income, employment status, loan amount, loan term and credit score are included. These features can be used to train machine learning models and predict the probability of loan default.

Guided Learning for Credit Risk Assessment

Supervised learning algorithms are often used in credit risk assessment when historical data with labelled outcomes (default or non-default) are available. Classification algorithms such as logistic regression, decision trees, random forests and gradient boosting machines (GBM) are used to predict the probability of loan default based on available features.

Unsupervised Learning to Assess Credit Risk

In situations where labelled information is scarce or unavailable, unsupervised learning methods can be used to assess credit risk. These techniques focus on finding patterns, clusters, and anomalies in data.

Clustering algorithms such as k-means clustering and hierarchical clustering group similar loan applicants based on their characteristics. This can help identify segments of borrowers with similar risk profiles, enabling more targeted risk analysis.

Outlier detection algorithms such as Isolation Forest and Local Outlier Factor detect unusual patterns or outliers in data. These deviations may indicate potential credit risks that require further investigation.

Evaluation Metrics for Credit Risk Assessment

Different metrics are used to evaluate the performance of credit risk assessment models. These metrics give an idea of how well the models predict the creditworthiness of loan applicants.

Table 2: Evaluation Metrics for Credit Risk Assessment

Metric	Formula
Accuracy	(True Positives + True Negatives) / Total Observations
Precision	True Positives / (True Positives + False Positives)
Recall	True Positives / (True Positives + False Negatives)
F1-score	2 * (Precision * Recall) / (Precision + Recall)
AUC-ROC	Area under the ROC curve

Table 2 shows the most commonly used rating measures for evaluating credit risk. Accuracy measures the overall accuracy of model predictions, accuracy quantifies the proportion of correctly identified subprime loans out of all predicted subprime cases, recall represents the proportion of correctly identified subprime loans out of all actual subprime loans, and the F1 score is a balance measure combining. accuracy and recall. The AUC-ROC metric analyzes the model's ability to discriminate between default and non-default cases.

In conclusion, machine learning techniques have revolutionized the loan approval process and credit risk assessment in the banking and finance industry. Data pre-processing and master planning ensure data quality and meaning. Supervised and unsupervised learning algorithms enable accurate risk assessment, while assessment metrics provide insight into model performance. By using these technologies, financial institutions can make informed loan approval decisions and effectively manage credit risk, resulting in more efficient and reliable lending practices.

4.5. ALGORITHMIC TRADING AND HIGH-FREQUENCY TRADING

Algorithmic Trading

Algorithmic trading refers to the use of computer algorithms to automate the trading process. These algorithms are designed to analyse market data, identify trading opportunities and execute trades based on predefined rules and strategies. Algorithmic trading has gained significant popularity in recent years due to its ability to remove human bias and emotion from trading decisions and make trading faster and more efficient.

Advantages of Algorithmic Trading

Algorithmic trading offers several advantages to traders and investors:

- **Speed and Efficiency:** Algorithms can process massive amounts of market data and execute trades in milliseconds, allowing traders to take advantage of market opportunities that appear and disappear quickly.
- **Accuracy:** Algorithmic trading eliminates potential human errors and emotional biases in trading decisions, resulting in more accurate and consistent trading.
- **Increased market liquidity:** Algorithmic trading can promote market liquidity by providing constant buying and selling. This benefits other market participants by ensuring continuous availability of liquidity.

4.5.2 Algorithmic Trading Strategies

Traders can use different algorithmic trading strategies depending on their goals and market conditions. Some of the most common algorithmic trading strategies include:

- **Momentum Trading:** This strategy identifies assets with significant price changes or strong momentum. Algorithms make trades to capture short-term price trends and build momentum.
- **Mean Reversion:** Mean reversion strategies use the idea that prices tend to move back to their average or mean after significant swings. Algorithms identify overbought or oversold assets and place trades to profit from the expected price change.
- **Statistical Arbitrage:** Statistical arbitrage strategies aim to exploit price inefficiencies in related securities. Algorithms identify pairs or groups of securities that historically move in sync but have temporarily deviated from their normal

relationship. Trades are made to take advantage of expected price convergence.

- **Ensure market emissions:** Market emissions algorithms provide liquidity to the market by constantly quoting both the buy and sell price of a certain set of securities. By providing liquidity, these algorithms win the bid-ask spread and help narrow the spread, which benefits other market participants.

Algorithmic Trading Techniques

Algorithmic trading is based on various technologies that enable efficient trading and market analysis. Some of the main techniques used in algorithmic trading are:

- **Data Feeds:** Live market data feeds provide traders with up-to-date information on prices, volumes and other relevant market variables. These data streams are crucial for algorithmic trading strategies to make informed trading decisions.
- **Execution Management Systems (EMS):** EMS platforms receive trading signals from algorithms and route orders to appropriate exchanges or trading venues for execution. EMS systems help optimize trade execution by connecting to multiple trading venues and routing orders based on factors such as price, liquidity and speed of execution.
- **Connectivity:** Fast internet connections and dedicated networks are crucial in algorithmic trading to ensure fast and reliable transmission of data between traders and exchanges. This helps minimize delays and ensures timely completion of transactions.

Now let's look at a table comparing different algorithmic trading strategies:

Table 1: Comparison of Algorithmic Trading Strategies

Strategy	Description	Example
Momentum Trading	Capitalizes on short-term price trends	Buying stocks that have recently surged in price
Mean Reversion	Takes advantage of price reversals after significant fluctuations	Buying oversold stocks and selling overbought stocks
Statistical Arbitrage	Exploits pricing inefficiencies between related securities	Pair trading, where long and short positions are taken in two correlated stocks
Market Making	Provides liquidity by continuously quoting bid and ask prices	Quoting bid and ask prices for a specific stock and earning the spread

The table compares different algorithmic trading strategies, highlighting their descriptions and examples. It introduces various strategies that can be used based on market conditions and business goals. Algorithmic trading has revolutionized the financial industry by enabling faster and more efficient trading, improving accuracy and promoting market liquidity. However, it is important for traders and market participants to develop sound strategies, conduct thorough testing and optimizations and ensure regulatory compliance in order to minimize risks and maximize the benefits of algorithmic trading.

4.6 HIGH FREQUENCY TRADING (HFT)

High Frequency Trading (HFT) is a subset of algorithmic trading that focuses on executing multiple trades in very short time periods, often measured in microseconds or milliseconds. HFT strategies aim to take advantage of small price differences and market inefficiencies that can be caused by various factors such as order imbalances, market news or temporary fluctuations of liquidity.

4.6.1 Advantages of High Frequency Trading

High frequency trading offers several advantages:

- **Speed:** HFT relies on very fast trading systems and low latency infrastructure to execute trades with minimal delay. The advantage of speed allows HFT firms to profit from small price changes and arbitrage opportunities that may exist for very short periods of time.
- **Liquidity:** HFT firms often act as liquidity providers in the market, constantly providing buy and sell prices. By providing liquidity, they reduce the bid-ask spread, increase market liquidity and facilitate trading by other market participants.
- **Market Efficiency:** HFT strategies contribute to market efficiency by quickly responding to price differences and reducing spreads. This reduces the impact of temporary price deviations and ensures the uniformity of the prices of different trading locations. 10.1.2 Challenges of High Frequency Trading

HFT Strategies Face Unique Challenges and Considerations

- **Technology and Infrastructure:** HFT requires significant investment in cutting-edge technology, high-speed connections and infrastructure to achieve the required speed and efficiency. This can include server colocation, proximity hosting, and specialized hardware such as field-programmable gate arrays (FPGAs) or application-specific integrated circuits (ASICs).

- **Regulatory Oversight:** HFT has attracted regulatory attention due to its potential impact on market integrity and market manipulation concerns. Regulatory authorities have taken steps to ensure a fair and orderly market, including rules on business practices, monitoring systems and risk management.
- **Risk management:** HFT strategies can be very sensitive to market conditions and if the algorithms or risk management processes are not reliable, there is a risk of loss. Risk management techniques such as position limits, real-time monitoring and risk management are crucial for reducing these risks.

High Frequency Trading Techniques

HFT relies on advanced technologies and infrastructure to support fast trading:

- **Low Latency Trading Systems:** HFT firms use powerful trading systems that can process massive amounts of data and execute trades in microseconds or milliseconds. These systems are designed to process market data, generate trading signals and execute trades quickly.
- **Direct Market Access (DMA):** DMA allows HFT firms to connect directly to exchanges and trading venues, bypassing intermediaries. By entering the market directly, HFT firms can reduce latency and improve transaction execution speed. 3. Market Data and Order Book Analysis: HFT strategies rely heavily on real-time market data feeds and advanced order book analysis. By monitoring order flows, liquidity imbalances and market microstructure, HFT algorithms can identify trading opportunities and execute trades quickly.
- **Organization and Proximity:** HFT firms often locate their servers near central data centres or use dedicated location services. This proximity reduces network latency and helps ensure faster data transfer and transaction execution.

Table 2: Comparison of Algorithmic Trading and High-Frequency Trading

Aspect	Algorithmic Trading	High-Frequency Trading
Timeframe	Medium to long-term	Ultra-short term
Trading Speed	Fast	Ultra-fast
Trade Frequency	Moderate	High
Trading Strategies	Diverse	Focus on low-latency strategies

Aspect	Algorithmic Trading	High-Frequency Trading
Market Impact	Moderate	Can have a significant impact
Infrastructure Needs	Moderate	Requires cutting-edge technology
Regulatory Scrutiny	Moderate	High

Table 2 provides a comparison between algorithmic trading and high-frequency trading, highlighting the differences in their schedules, trading speed, trading frequency, trading strategies, market impact, infrastructure needs and regulatory oversight. Although both strategies use automation and algorithms, HFT focuses on very fast, high-frequency trading, with a special emphasis on low-latency strategies.

High Frequency Trading has revolutionized the trading environment, bringing unprecedented speed and liquidity to the market. However, it is a complex and highly competitive industry that requires significant investments in technology and infrastructure. It is essential that high-speed trading firms develop strong risk management frameworks, adhere to regulatory guidelines and continuously innovate to stay ahead of the curve in the fast-paced world of high-speed trading.

5

Industrial and Manufacturing Processes Using Machine Learning

5.1. INTRODUCTION OF ML APPLICATIONS IN MANUFACTURING AND INDUSTRY

Machine learning (ML) has significantly impacted the manufacturing and industrial sectors, enabling advanced analytics, automation and optimization. ML applications in manufacturing and industry cover many areas, including predictive maintenance, quality control, supply chain optimization, and process optimization. These applications use ML algorithms to analyze large volumes of data, identify patterns, make predictions and optimize operations to improve efficiency, productivity and cost-effectiveness.

1. Preventive Maintenance

Predictive maintenance is an ML application that uses data analysis techniques to predict when equipment is likely to fail or require maintenance. Traditional maintenance strategies often involve regular periodic maintenance or reactive maintenance when failure occurs. However, these methods can be expensive and ineffective. The goal of preventive maintenance is to optimize maintenance schedules by identifying the optimal maintenance based on equipment condition and performance data.

Data Collection and Tracking: When implementing proactive maintenance, data collection and tracking are critical. Data on device sensors such as temperature, pressure, vibration or energy consumption are continuously collected and monitored in real time. This information, along with other relevant usage data, is used to create predictive models that can detect patterns, anomalies and degradation of device performance.

Construction of predictive models: Machine learning algorithms are used to build predictive models to predict equipment failures. These models analyze historical sensor data, maintenance logs and other related data to identify patterns and correlations between various parameters and equipment failures. Common ML algorithms used for predictive maintenance include regression models, decision trees, random forests, and neural networks.

Benefits of preventive maintenance

Proactive maintenance offers several benefits to manufacturing organizations, including:

- **Reduced downtime:** By predicting equipment failures, preventive maintenance can be planned, minimizing unexpected downtime and production interruptions.
- **Cost savings:** Proactive maintenance helps optimize maintenance activities, reduce unnecessary maintenance and minimize equipment damage. This results in savings on maintenance resources, spare parts and equipment repairs.
- **Better efficiency:** By performing maintenance at the optimal time, the efficiency and performance of equipment can be improved, which increases productivity and reduces energy consumption.
- **Better safety:** Proactive maintenance helps identify potential safety risks and allows for timely maintenance measures to ensure a safe working environment.
- **Extend the useful life of equipment:** The useful life of equipment can be extended by monitoring the condition of equipment and solving problems quickly, which reduces the need for premature replacements.
- **Better planning and resource allocation:** Predictive maintenance provides information about the condition and performance of equipment, enabling better planning of maintenance schedules, resource allocation and inventory management.

In summary, predictive maintenance uses ML algorithms to predict equipment failures, enabling predictive maintenance planning. This approach minimizes downtime, reduces maintenance costs and optimizes the life of the machines. By using data analytics, manufacturing organizations can make their operations more efficient, improve equipment reliability and reduce maintenance costs.

2. Quality Control

Quality control involves monitoring and inspecting products at various stages of the production process to ensure that they meet predefined quality standards. Traditionally, quality control has been based on manual inspection, which can be time-consuming, subjective and prone to human error. ML algorithms have revolutionized quality control by automating the inspection process, enabling faster and more accurate defect detection and classification.

Detection of defects: ML algorithms can analyze images, sensor data, or other related data sources to identify defects in manufactured products. By training ML models on large datasets containing examples of both faulty and defective products, the algorithms learn to identify patterns and anomalies associated with defects. During an inspection, these models can quickly analyze images or sensor readings and identify any deviations from expected quality standards.

Classification of defects: In addition to detecting defects, ML algorithms can classify the nature and severity of defects. Using deep learning techniques such as Convolutional Neural Networks (CNN), ML models can learn to classify defects into specific classes based on visual features. This allows manufacturers to understand the types of defects that occur and take the necessary steps to correct them.

Table 1: Quality Control Considerations

Consideration	Description
Defect Detection	Employing ML algorithms to automatically detect anomalies and defects in manufactured products.
Defect Classification	Utilizing ML to classify defects into specific categories based on visual characteristics.
Real-Time Quality Assessment	Performing real-time monitoring and assessment of product quality during the manufacturing process.
Process Improvement	Analyzing quality data to identify patterns, correlations, and root causes for process optimization.

ML applications have greatly improved manufacturing quality control by automating defect detection, classification and real-time quality assessment. By utilizing ML algorithms, manufacturers can improve the efficiency and accuracy of quality control processes, minimize defective products, and improve overall product quality. This increases customer satisfaction, lowers costs and improves competitiveness in the market.

3. Supply chain optimization

Supply chain optimization involves the use of machine learning algorithms to improve various parts of the supply chain, including demand forecasting, inventory management and logistics planning. By leveraging historical data, market trends and external factors, machine learning models can create accurate forecasts, optimize inventory levels and streamline logistics operations.

Forecast: Forecasting is an important part of supply chain optimization. Machine learning algorithms can analyze historical sales data, market trends and other relevant factors to produce accurate demand forecasts. These forecasts help manufacturers and retailers anticipate customer demand, plan production schedules and optimize inventory. By better understanding future demand, companies can minimize inventory, reduce excess inventory and improve customer satisfaction.

Inventory management: Optimizing inventory levels is very important to achieve cost-effective operation of the supply chain. Machine learning algorithms can analyze demand patterns, sales data and other factors to determine optimal inventory. By avoiding over- and under-stocking, companies can reduce costs, avoid inventory and improve overall warehouse efficiency. ML algorithms can also provide insight into restocking strategies and identify optimal reorder points and quantities to balance inventory.

Table 2: Supply Chain Optimization Components

Component	Description
Demand Forecasting	Utilizing machine learning algorithms to generate accurate predictions of customer demand.
Inventory Management	Optimizing inventory levels to balance customer demand and minimize carrying costs.
Logistics Optimization	Enhancing transportation, warehousing, and distribution processes to improve efficiency and reduce costs.
Supplier Management	Analyzing supplier data to optimize supplier selection, performance, and quality.

In conclusion, supply chain optimization using machine learning enables companies to make data-driven decisions, improve efficiency, lower costs and improve customer satisfaction. By accurately forecasting demand, optimizing inventory levels and streamlining logistics operations, companies can achieve a more flexible and responsive supply chain. ML algorithms provide valuable insights and recommendations that help companies adapt to market dynamics, minimize risk and gain competitive advantage in the dynamic environment of modern supply chains.

4. Process Optimization

Process optimization uses machine learning algorithms to analyze sensor data, operating parameters and historical process data to improve the efficiency, quality and productivity of manufacturing processes. By utilizing ML techniques, manufacturers can identify patterns, correlations and optimization opportunities that can lead to significant improvements in various aspects of their operations.

Data Collection and Tracking: In order to optimize production processes, it is important to collect and verify relevant information from various sources. This includes data from sensors embedded in machines, production lines and other equipment, as well as data on operating parameters such as temperature, pressure and speed. Real-time data collection enables continuous monitoring and analysis, enabling the rapid identification of anomalies or deviations that may affect the process.

Data analysis and pattern recognition: Once the data is collected, machine learning algorithms can be applied to analyze the data and identify patterns and correlations. By identifying patterns in data, ML models can reveal insights that may not be obvious to human observers. This knowledge can be used to understand the relationships between process parameters and performance indicators, leading to the identification of optimization opportunities.

Table 3: Key Elements of Process Optimization

Elements	Description
Data Collection and Monitoring	Collecting and monitoring data from sensors and operational parameters.
Data Analysis and Pattern Recognition	Analyzing data to identify patterns, correlations, and optimization opportunities.
Optimization Algorithms and Techniques	Utilizing ML algorithms to develop optimization models and search for optimal solutions.
Anomaly Detection and Fault Diagnosis	Using ML to detect anomalies and diagnose faults in manufacturing processes.
Continuous Improvement and Adaptive Control	Iteratively improving processes based on feedback and adapting to changing conditions.

In conclusion, process optimization in industry and manufacturing involves the use of ML techniques in data analysis, identify patterns and optimize process parameters. With continuous monitoring and data analysis, manufacturers can achieve greater efficiency, productivity and quality in their operations. ML algorithms make it possible to discover optimization opportunities, identify anomalies, identify failures and adjust control, improving the overall performance and operation of the process.

In summary, ML applications have revolutionized the manufacturing and industrial sectors by enabling predictive maintenance, quality control, supply chain optimization and process optimization. By utilizing ML algorithms, manufacturers can make informed decisions, improve labour efficiency, reduce costs and improve product quality. These applications pave the way to a more streamlined, automated and intelligent manufacturing industry.

5.2. DEFECT DETECTION AND QUALITY CONTROL

Defect detection and quality control are critical processes in manufacturing to ensure that products meet the required standards and specifications. Machine learning techniques have revolutionized defect detection and quality control by automating the process, improving accuracy, and enabling real-time monitoring. Let's explore some key aspects of this topic:

1. Image-Based Defect Detection

Image-based defect detection involves analyzing images or visual data to identify defects or anomalies in products or components. Machine learning algorithms such as Convolutional Neural Networks (CNN) are widely used in image analysis. These algorithms are trained on labelled datasets where images are classified as defective or non-defective. By learning patterns and features from these labelled images, the ML model can accurately classify new images and highlight potential defects. Image-based defect detection is particularly useful in industries such as manufacturing, where visual inspection is a common method of quality control.

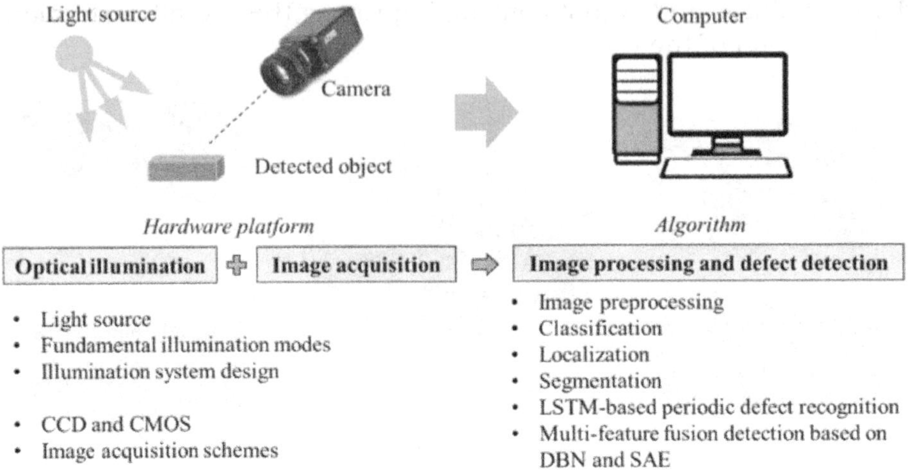

Image-Based Defect Detection

Acquisition and pre-processing of images: The first step in image-based fault detection is to obtain high-quality images of products or components. This can be done with cameras or other imaging devices strategically placed on the production line. It is important to ensure that the images capture the important features and details needed to identify the fault.

Once images are acquired, pre-processing techniques can be used to improve image quality and suitability for analysis. This may include tasks such as image resizing, noise reduction and contrast enhancement to improve the clarity and visibility of any defects.

Preparation of training data: Image-based error detection requires large labeled data to train a machine learning model. This dataset consists of images of both normal and defective products with annotations indicating the presence and location of defects. The dataset should cover a wide range of fault types and variations to ensure that the model is effective in detecting different types of faults.

Training data preparation involves careful image curation and annotation, ensuring accurate labeling of errors. This step is crucial because the quality and diversity of the training data directly affects the performance of the machine learning model.

Convolutional Neural Networks (CNN): Convolutional Neural Networks (CNN) are widely used for image-based defect detection due to their ability to learn and extract important features from images. CNNs are designed to automatically learn hierarchical representations of image data, capture low-level features such as edges and textures, and progressively combine them to identify higher-level patterns and structures.

Training a CNN model involves feeding labeled training data to the network and iteratively adjusting its parameters to minimize the difference between predicted and actual error labels. The model learns to recognize unique patterns and characteristics associated with different types of defects, enabling accurate classification.

Identification and classification of defects: Once a CNN model is trained, it can be used to detect and classify errors in real time. The model takes an input image, processes it through the layers of the network, and creates a prediction that indicates the presence or absence of defects. If a fault is detected, the model can also provide information about the type or category of the fault.

Defect detection using CNNs is a very accurate and efficient process. By analyzing images at high speed, the model quickly detects defects, allowing manufacturers to take immediate corrective action and minimize the production of defective products.

Table 3: Image-Based Defect Detection Process

Process Step	Description
Image Acquisition and Pre-processing	Capturing high-quality images of products and performing necessary pre-processing techniques.
Training Data Preparation	Curating and annotating a diverse dataset of labeled images for training the CNN model.
Convolutional Neural Networks	Training a CNN model to learn and extract meaningful features from the labeled training data.
Defect Detection and Classification	Using the trained CNN model to detect and classify defects in real-time images.

2. Sensor-Based Defect Detection

Sensor-based defect detection is a technique used in industry and manufacturing to identify and classify defects or anomalies by analyzing data from sensors embedded in production equipment. These sensors measure various parameters such as temperature, pressure, vibration or electrical signals, providing valuable information about the quality and performance of the production process. Using machine learning algorithms, manufacturers can effectively identify and correct defects in real time, improve product quality and minimize manufacturing errors.

Here are the main considerations and steps for sensor-based troubleshooting.

- **Data collection:** Sensors are strategically placed on manufacturing equipment to collect data during the manufacturing process. These sensors continuously measure relevant parameters and generate a data stream.
- **Data pre-processing:** The collected sensor data is pre-processed to remove noise, handle missing values and, if necessary, normalize the data. Preprocessing ensures data analysis and improves the accuracy of problem-solving algorithms.
- **Feature Extraction:** Machine learning algorithms require meaningful features to identify patterns and anomalies. Feature extraction involves transforming sensor data into meaningful representations that store meaningful information. This step helps reduce the dimensionality of the data and highlight important patterns.
- **Training data preparation:** Annotated training data is required to train machine learning models. This includes manual inspection and labeling of defective and damaged products or processes. The labeled data serves as a reference for the machine learning algorithm to learn patterns and make accurate predictions.
- **Model Training:** Machine learning algorithms such as anomaly detection algorithms or classification algorithms are trained using labeled training data. The algorithm learns to distinguish between normal and faulty process behavior based on data patterns.
- **Anomaly detection or classification:** Once the model is trained, it can be used to analyze new sensor data in real time. Anomaly detection algorithms detect deviations or deviations from normal sensor readings that indicate the presence of faults or anomalies. Classification algorithms classify data into different categories, such as defective or non-defective, based on learned patterns.

Real-time Monitoring and Alarms

A trained model is used to continuously monitor sensor data during the production process. Any anomalies or deviations detected by the model will trigger alarms or notifications to users or control systems. This allows timely intervention and corrective action to prevent the production of defective products.

By using sensor-based error detection with machine learning, manufacturers can achieve the following benefits.

- **Real-time Defect Detection:** Defects can be detected as soon as they occur, enabling immediate corrective action and minimizing the production of defective products.
- **Improved quality control:** Continuous monitoring of sensor data ensures consistent quality control throughout the manufacturing process, improving product quality and customer satisfaction.
- **Cost reduction:** Early detection of defects reduces waste, rework and scrap, resulting in cost savings for manufacturers.
- **Process Optimization:** By analyzing sensor data, manufacturers can identify areas for process improvement and optimize parameters to avoid defects.
- **Predictive maintenance:** Sensor data can also be used for predictive maintenance, where abnormal readings can indicate potential equipment failures or maintenance requirements, enabling proactive maintenance and minimizing downtime.

3. Quality Control and Statistical Process Control (SPC)

Quality control is an important part of production processes to ensure that products meet the desired quality standards. Statistical Process Control (SPC) is a technique used in quality control to monitor and control the quality of production processes using statistical methods. Machine learning algorithms can play a valuable role in improving SPC by analyzing process data, identifying patterns or anomalies, and providing insights for proactive quality management.

- **Collection and Tracking of Data:** The first step in quality control and SPC is to collect and control the necessary data from the production process. This includes information such as dimensions, weight, temperature or other process variables that can affect product quality. Automated data collection systems can collect real-time data from sensors or measuring devices, ensuring accurate and timely data for analysis.
- **Statistical analysis and control charts:** Statistical analysis is an integral part of the Summary of Product Characteristics. Machine learning algorithms can be used to analyze process data, identify trends, variations and patterns and generate control charts. Control charts are graphical representations of process data over time, including control limits that define acceptable ranges. By comparing the data with the control limits, manufacturers can determine if the process is in statistical control or if there are signs of special causes or quality problems.

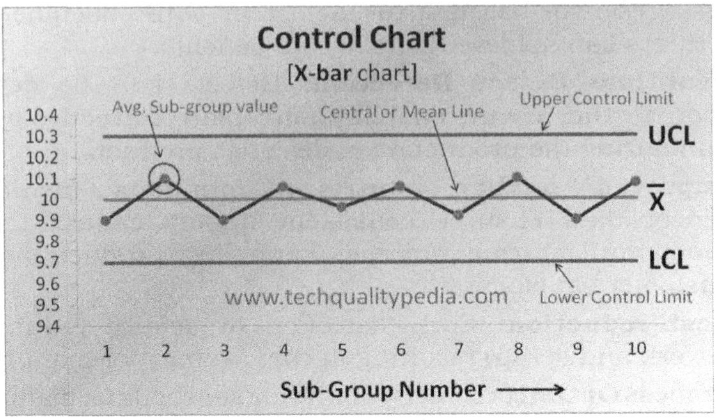

Statistical Process Control (SPC)

Deviation detection and root cause analysis: Machine learning algorithms can help detect anomalies by identifying data points that fall outside control limits or exhibit unusual patterns. These deviations may indicate potential quality problems or process deviations that require investigation. ML models can be trained to distinguish between normal process variations and abnormal conditions, enabling early detection of quality problems. Root cause analysis methods combined with ML algorithms can help identify contributing factors to quality problems and facilitate targeted corrective actions.

Proactive analysis and process improvement: Machine learning algorithms can also be used for predictive analytics in quality control. By analyzing historical process data, ML models can predict future quality problems or defects, enabling proactive action. Predictive analytics can help manufacturers identify critical process parameters, optimize process settings, and make informed decisions to improve product quality and reduce defects. ML algorithms can continuously learn from new data, refine predictive models and drive continuous process improvement.

Table 4: Key Elements of Quality Control and SPC

Elements	Description
Data Collection and Monitoring	Collecting and monitoring process data, including dimensions, weights, temperatures, etc.
Statistical Analysis and Control Charts	Analyzing data and generating control charts to monitor process performance.
Anomaly Detection and Root Cause Analysis	Detecting anomalies and investigating the root causes of quality issues.
Predictive Analytics and Process Improvement	Utilizing ML for predictive modeling, process optimization, and continuous improvement.

In summary, defect detection and quality control are key areas in manufacturing processes. Machine learning techniques, including image-based defect detection, sensor-based defect detection, and quality control techniques such as statistical process control, enable manufacturers to identify and solve quality problems in real time. By leveraging ML algorithms, manufacturers can improve product quality, reduce defects, and improve overall customer satisfaction.

5.3. EQUIPMENT FAILURE PREDICTION AND PREDICTIVE MAINTENANCE

Equipment failure can lead to costly production downtime, reduced productivity and increased maintenance costs. Predictive maintenance based on machine learning algorithms aims to prevent equipment failures before they occur, enabling proactive maintenance measures to minimize disruptions and optimize maintenance schedules.

1. Data collection and integration of sensors

Data collection includes the collection of relevant data from sensors installed in the device. These sensors are strategically placed to monitor various parameters such as temperature, vibration, pressure or electrical signals. The collected information provides an overview of the health, performance and condition of the devices. The data collection and sensor integration process include the following steps.

Sensor placement: Sensors are strategically placed on the device to collect data related to its operating parameters. Different types of sensors are used depending on the monitored parameters. For example, temperature sensors can be placed in critical locations to monitor temperature fluctuations, while vibration sensors can be attached to rotating machinery to monitor vibration levels.

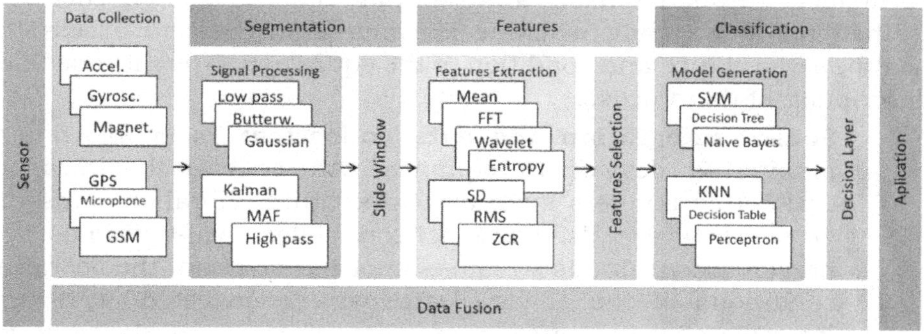

Data collection and integration of sensors

- **Real-time data collection:** Sensors continuously collect real-time data. Data is usually collected at regular intervals, which provides a continuous flow of information about the condition of the device. Collected data can be stored locally on devices or transferred to a centralized data storage system for further analysis.
- **Data pre-processing:** Before analysis, the collected data can be pre-processed to ensure their quality and usability. This may involve cleaning, filtering, normalization or de-outliering to remove noise or inconsistencies in the data. Preprocessing helps improve the accuracy and reliability of subsequent analyses.
- **Data integration:** In addition to sensor data, other relevant data sources can be integrated to obtain a complete picture of device performance. This may include historical maintenance data, environmental data, usage data or data about other related equipment or processes. The integration of multiple data sources enriches the analysis and enables a more comprehensive understanding of device behaviour.
- **Information storage and management:** Collected and pre-processed information is stored in a centralized database or information management system. It enables easy data access, retrieval and analysis using machine learning algorithms or predictive maintenance software.

By integrating sensors and collecting real-time data, manufacturers can gain valuable information about equipment operating conditions, performance trends and potential failure indicators. This information is the basis for subsequent analysis using machine learning algorithms.

2. Condition monitoring and data analysis

Condition monitoring includes continuous monitoring of device parameters through sensors and real-time data collection. This data is then analyzed using machine learning algorithms to assess the health, performance and condition of the equipment. Here is a detailed description of the process:

- **Sensor integration and data collection:** To enable fitness monitoring, devices are equipped with sensors that measure various parameters such as temperature, vibration, pressure or electrical signals. These sensors collect real-time data and provide a continuous stream of information about the operating conditions of the device. Data can be collected at regular intervals or transmitted in real time to a central database for analysis.

Pre-processing of data: Before data analysis, pre-processing of the collected data is required. This step involves cleaning the data, removing outliers or noise, and handling missing values. Data preprocessing ensures that the data used for analysis is accurate and reliable, which improves the quality of subsequent machine learning models.

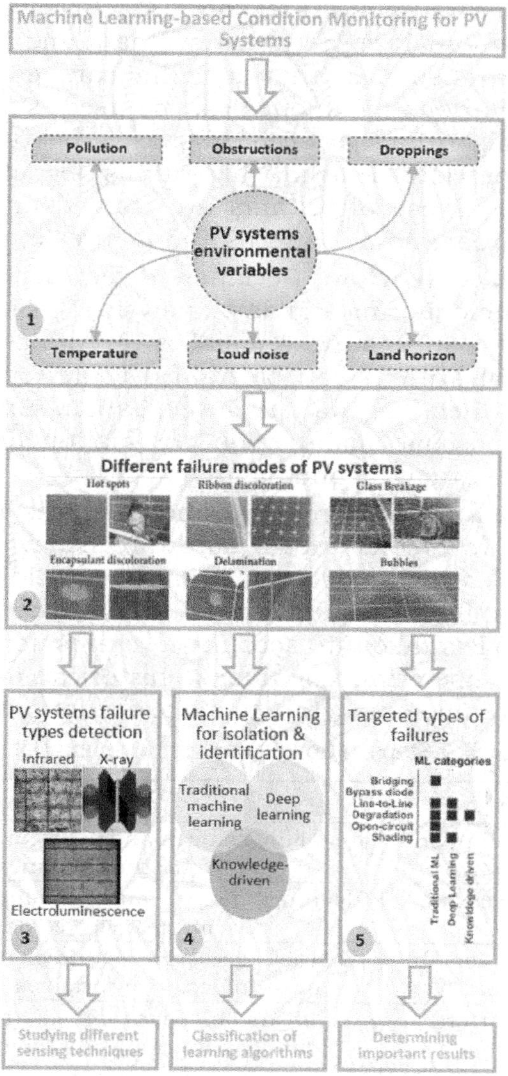

Condition monitoring

- **Deleting and Selecting Features:** In exercise tracking, important features or characteristics are extracted from raw sensor data. Feature extraction involves transforming raw data into meaningful representations that capture important patterns or information. Then, feature selection techniques are applied to identify the most informative and meaningful features of the predictive models. This helps reduce the complexity of the calculation and focuses on the most influential variables.

- **Algorithms for machine learning:** Machine learning algorithms are used to analyze pre-processed data and identify patterns, trends or anomalies that may indicate potential hardware failures. Various techniques can be used, such as supervised learning algorithms (eg decision trees, support vector machines) or unsupervised learning algorithms (eg clustering, outlier detection). These algorithms are trained on historical data, learning from known patterns and failures to predict new data.
- **Deviation detection:** Deviation detection is a key part of condition monitoring and data analysis. This includes detecting abnormal patterns or anomalies in device data. Machine learning algorithms can be trained to detect these anomalies and flag them for further investigation. Abnormalities may indicate possible malfunctions or malfunctions that require immediate attention and maintenance.
- **Proactive Analysis:** Predictive analytics uses insights from data analytics to predict future hardware behaviour and failures. Machine learning models built on historical data can estimate the probability of equipment failure in a certain time period. These models take into account several factors such as sensor readings, operating conditions, historical maintenance data and environmental factors to make accurate predictions.

Table 5: Key Steps in Condition Monitoring and Data Analysis

Steps	Description
Sensor Integration and Data Collection	Installing sensors and collecting real-time data from the equipment.
Data Preprocessing	Cleaning, filtering, and handling missing values in the collected data.
Feature Extraction and Selection	Extracting relevant features and selecting the most informative variables for analysis.
Machine Learning Algorithms	Applying ML algorithms to analyze the data, identify patterns, and predict equipment failures.
Anomaly Detection	Detecting abnormal patterns or deviations from normal behavior in the equipment data.
Predictive Analytics	Using historical data and ML models to forecast future equipment behavior and predict failures.

3. Predictive models and failure prediction

Predictive models play an important role in equipment failure prediction and preventive maintenance. These models use machine learning algorithms to analyze historical data, identify patterns and predict the probability of equipment failure. Using advanced technologies, these models provide valuable information about potential failures, which enables preventive maintenance measures.

- **Selection of functions and data processing:** Before building predictive models, it is important to select relevant characteristics or variables that significantly affect equipment condition and performance. These characteristics may include sensor readings, operating conditions, maintenance history, environmental factors, or other relevant parameters. Data preparation techniques such as data cleaning, normalization, and feature planning are used to ensure high quality data for model training.
- **Model training and evaluation:** Machine learning algorithms are used to train predictive models using historical data. Various algorithms can be used, such as decision trees, random forests, support vector machines (SVM) or recurrent neural networks (RNN). During training, models learn patterns and relationships between selected features and faults. The models are then evaluated using appropriate metrics such as precision, accuracy, recall, or area under the receiver operating curve (ROC) to assess their performance.

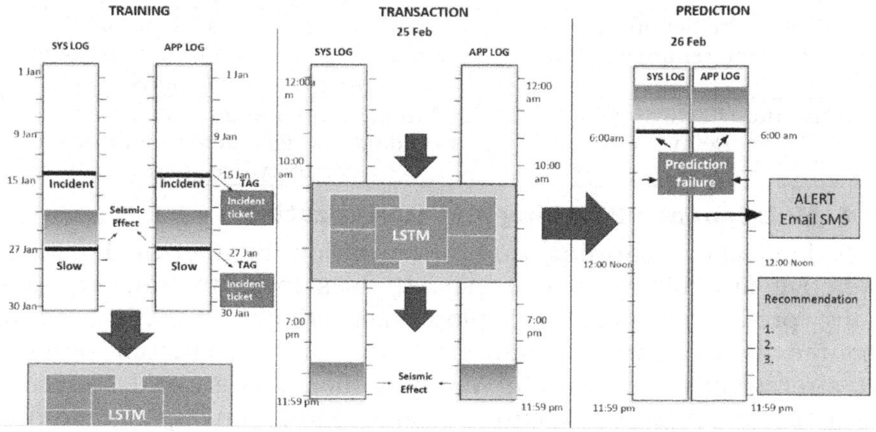

Failure Prediction

- **Prediction of failures and preventive maintenance measures:** Once trained and evaluated, predictive models can be used to predict equipment failures. These models take into account current operating conditions and historical data to calculate the probability of failure over a period of time. If the predicted probability exceeds a certain threshold, it means an increased probability of failure. Based on these forecasts, preventive maintenance actions can be initiated, such as scheduling inspections, replacing critical components, or scheduling downtime for repairs.
- **Continuous learning and model improvement:** Forecasting models are not static entities. They can be continuously refined and improved based on new information and feedback from actual maintenance procedures. By training models with regularly updated data, the models can adapt to changing conditions, incorporate new failure patterns, and improve their accuracy over time. This continuous learning ensures that predictive models remain relevant and effective in identifying potential equipment failures.

Table 6: Key Aspects of Predictive Models and Failure Prediction

Aspects	Description
Feature Selection and Data Preparation	Selecting relevant features and preparing the data for model training and evaluation.
Model Training and Evaluation	Utilizing machine learning algorithms to train predictive models and evaluating their performance.
Failure Prediction and Proactive Maintenance Actions	Using the trained models to predict equipment failures and initiate proactive maintenance actions.
Continuous Learning and Model Refinement	Updating and refining the models based on new data and feedback to improve their accuracy over time.

4. Maintenance Planning and Optimization

Maintenance planning and optimization is a critical aspect of predictive maintenance strategies. It uses insights from equipment failure prediction models to plan maintenance activities, optimize resource allocation and minimize disruptions to production processes. By strategically scheduling maintenance tasks and prioritizing resources, manufacturers can maximize equipment uptime, minimize costs, and improve overall operational efficiency.

- **Optimization of the maintenance schedule:** Predictive maintenance allows manufacturers to move away from traditional calendar-based maintenance schedules to condition-based or predictive schedules. Instead of maintenance work performed at fixed intervals, maintenance activities are scheduled based on the expected condition and condition of the equipment. By considering factors such as equipment performance, historical data, and predicted failure probabilities, maintenance schedules can be optimized to minimize downtime and maximize the use of maintenance resources.

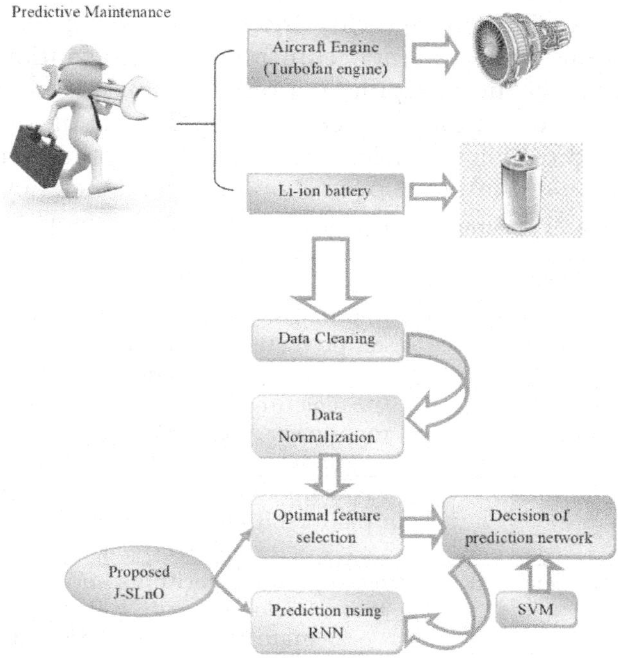

Maintenance planning

- **Resource allocation and planning:** Effective maintenance planning requires efficient allocation of resources such as labour, spare parts and tools. Predictive maintenance models provide insight into expected maintenance needs and schedules, allowing manufacturers to allocate resources accordingly. By accurately predicting failure events and planning maintenance activities in advance, manufacturers can ensure that the necessary resources are available when needed, reducing delays and improving maintenance efficiency.
- **Cost optimization:** Maintenance planning and optimization also focuses on cost reduction. By implementing proactive maintenance strategies, manufacturers can avoid costly

unplanned downtime and emergency repairs. Predictive models provide early warning signs of equipment failure, enabling preventive maintenance during scheduled maintenance periods. This approach minimizes the impact on production schedules and reduces the need for costly fixes or replacements.

- **Maintenance decision support systems:** Machine learning algorithms and predictive maintenance models can be integrated into maintenance decision support systems. These systems provide maintenance teams with real-time insights and recommendations, allowing them to make informed decisions. Maintenance personnel can receive information about the condition of the equipment, predicted failure probabilities and recommended maintenance actions. This enables them to make informed decisions, prioritize tasks and optimize maintenance operations to improve overall operational efficiency.

Table 7: Maintenance Planning and Optimization Techniques

Techniques	Description
Maintenance Schedule Optimization	Optimizing maintenance schedules based on predicted equipment health and failure probabilities.
Resource Allocation and Planning	Efficiently allocating resources such as manpower, spare parts, and tools based on maintenance needs and priorities.
Cost Optimization	Reducing maintenance costs by minimizing unplanned downtime, emergency repairs, and expedited replacements.
Maintenance Decision Support Systems	Integrating ML algorithms and predictive models into decision support systems for informed maintenance decision-making.

In short, equipment failure prediction and predictive maintenance enable proactive maintenance actions based on data-driven insights. Using machine learning algorithms, manufacturers can analyze sensor data, predict failures and optimize maintenance schedules. This approach minimizes unplanned downtime, lowers maintenance costs and improves overall equipment reliability and efficiency.

6

Machine Learning in Robotics and Autonomous Systems

6.1 INTRODUCTION TO ROBOTICS AND AUTONOMOUS SYSTEMS

The fields of robotics and autonomous systems merge ideas from engineering, computer science, and artificial intelligence. Robots and autonomous systems can observe and interact with their surroundings, make informed decisions, and learn from their experiences thanks to machine learning, a branch of artificial intelligence.

The relationship between robotics, autonomous systems, and machine learning will be examined in this article, with a focus on key ideas, applications, and methodologies.

Robotics and Autonomous Systems Overview

Robotics and Autonomous Systems (RAS) is a rapidly developing field that combines machine learning and robotics to develop intelligent systems that can perform tasks autonomously. Machine learning plays a key role in RAS because it enables robots to learn from data, adapt to their environment and make informed decisions. Using algorithms and models, robots can perceive, reason and act in real-world scenarios without human intervention.

RAS uses machine learning techniques to teach robots to recognize and understand their environment. It involves processing sensory inputs such as images, videos and sensor data to extract meaningful information from the environment. Deep learning models allow robots to recognize objects, detect obstacles and analyze complex scenes. This perception allows them to navigate independently, manipulate objects and interact with people safely and effectively.

Another important aspect of RAS is the ability to make informed decisions based on acquired information. Machine learning algorithms allow robots to learn from past experiences and optimize their behavior accordingly. For example, reinforcement learning techniques allow robots to learn through trial and error and receive feedback and rewards for their actions. This iterative learning process allows robots to improve their performance over time, adapt to changing conditions and become more efficient and reliable.

The applications of RAS and machine learning are wide and varied. These range from autonomous vehicles and drones that manage traffic and avoid collisions to industrial robots that automate manufacturing processes with precision and efficiency. In health care, RAS can help in surgery, rehabilitation and elderly care, improving the quality and safety of medical procedures. In addition, RAS can be used in, for example, agriculture, logistics, search and rescue, and space exploration.

Overall, the integration of machine learning techniques into robotics and autonomous systems has revolutionized the way robots interact and navigate the world. Using data-driven approaches, robots can increasingly perceive, learn and act autonomously, leading to advances in various fields and paving the way to a future where intelligent robotic systems are an integral part of our daily lives.

Role of Machine Learning in Robotics and Autonomous Systems

Machine learning plays a crucial role in robotics and autonomous systems, as they are able to perceive, reason and act intelligently in complex and dynamic environments. Using data-driven algorithms, machine learning enables robots and autonomous systems to learn from their experiences, adapt to changing circumstances and make informed decisions.

One of the main applications of machine learning in robotics is perception. Equipped with sensors such as cameras, lidar and sonar, robots generate vast amounts of information about their environment. Machine learning algorithms can analyze this data to derive relevant information such as object detection, scene understanding, and depth estimation. By learning patterns and features from labeled or unlabeled data, robots can accurately perceive their environment and make informed decisions based on the information obtained.

Another important aspect where machine learning excels in robotics is motion planning and control. Autonomous systems must navigate and communicate effectively in their environment. Machine learning algorithms can analyze the environment, past experiences and sensor data to learn optimal driving strategies. For example, reinforcement learning techniques allow robots to learn through trial and error, improving their ability to plan and execute complex tasks. This allows robots to adapt their movements and actions based on the information they learn, resulting in more efficient and effective performance.

Machine learning also promotes the development of autonomous decision-making systems. Autonomous systems often face uncertainty, unpredictable scenarios and dynamic environments. By combining machine learning algorithms, robots can learn from historical data, identify patterns and make future predictions. This enables them to make intelligent decisions and take necessary actions in real time, ensuring security, efficiency and adaptability. In addition, machine learning improves human-robot communication and collaboration. Using natural language processing and computer vision technology, robots can understand and interpret human commands, gestures and expressions. By analyzing human behavior and communication patterns, bots can adjust their responses and actions accordingly, making communication more intuitive and fluid.

Table 1: Examples of Robotics and Autonomous Systems Applications

Application	Description
Industrial Robotics	Deployed in manufacturing environments for tasks like assembly, welding, and material handling.
Autonomous Vehicles	Self-driving cars, drones, and agricultural robots for transportation and surveillance purposes.
Healthcare Robotics	Assisting with surgeries, patient care, and rehabilitation.
Search and Rescue	Robots used in disaster-stricken areas for locating and rescuing survivors.
Service Robotics	Robots for household chores, elderly care, and hospitality.

Machine Learning Techniques in Robotics and Autonomous Systems:

Machine learning techniques have revolutionized the field of robotics and autonomous systems, enabling machines to acquire information, adapt to their environment and make intelligent decisions. In the context of robotics, machine learning algorithms are used to process large amounts of sensor data, extract meaningful patterns, and learn complex patterns that can be used for detection, control, and decision making.

One of the main applications of machine learning in robotics is perception. Robots are equipped with various sensors, such as cameras, lidars and radars, which collect information about their environment. Machine learning algorithms such as Convolutional Neural Networks (CNNs) and Recurrent Neural Networks (RNNs) can be trained using labeled data to detect objects, detect obstacles, and interpret scenes. Using deep learning techniques, robots can develop a comprehensive understanding of their environment, allowing them to navigate safely and interact with objects efficiently.

Machine learning also plays a crucial role in robot control. For example, reinforcement learning (RL) algorithms can be used to teach robots to perform tasks through trial and error. By providing rewards or punishments based on the robot's actions, RL algorithms can optimize the robot's behavior over time, allowing it to learn complex motor skills and skillfully manipulate objects. This has a significant impact on, for example, the manipulation, grasping and movement of the robot. In addition, machine learning facilitates decision making in autonomous systems. Autonomous robots often operate in dynamic and uncertain environments, forcing them to make real-time decisions based on changing conditions. Using techniques such as Bayesian inference, probabilistic modeling and deep learning, robots can learn to make informed decisions under uncertainty. These algorithms allow robots to plan optimal paths, navigate complex terrain and respond to unexpected events, ensuring robust and adaptive behavior.

Table 2: Machine Learning Techniques in Robotics and Autonomous Systems

Technique	Description
Reinforcement Learning	Agents learn through interaction with the environment and rewards/punishments.
Supervised Learning	Training models with labeled data to make predictions or classifications.
Unsupervised Learning	Discovering patterns and structures in data without explicit labels.
Deep Learning	Neural networks with multiple layers used for complex pattern recognition.
Computer Vision	Techniques for perceiving and interpreting visual information.
Natural Language Processing	Enabling robots to understand and generate human language.

Challenges and Future Directions

Machine learning has revolutionized many fields, from computer vision and natural language processing to healthcare and finance. However, there are still many challenges and many future directions in the field of machine learning that researchers are actively working on.

One of the major challenges of machine learning is the scarcity of data. Many machine learning algorithms require large amounts of labeled data to achieve high accuracy. But obtaining tag data can be time-consuming, expensive or even impractical in certain industries. Meeting this challenge requires the development of knowledge augmentation, transfer, and semi-supervised learning techniques that aim to exploit limited labeled data using auxiliary information or unlabeled data.

Another challenge is the interpretability of machine learning models. As deep learning models become increasingly sophisticated, they often act as black boxes, making it difficult to understand the reasoning behind their predictions. This lack of interpretability can be particularly problematic in critical areas such as health care or finance, where decisions must be justified. Researchers are actively exploring the methods of explainability and interpretability of models with the goal of providing insight into the inner workings of complex models and increasing confidence in their decisions. The problem of machine learning biases is also a big problem. Machine learning models learn from historical data that may contain social biases. Partisan models can perpetuate and reinforce existing social, gender, or racial biases, leading to unjust outcomes. To address this challenge, researchers are focusing on developing algorithms that tolerate bias, collect diverse and representative data sets, and apply fairness metrics to ensure fair decision making.

Another area of interest is lifelong learning, or continuous learning, where machine learning models can adapt over time and learn from new data without forgetting previously learned information. This skill is crucial because the world is dynamic and models must constantly update their knowl edge. Continuous learning involves catastrophic forgetting, which occurs when a model trained on new data forgets previously learne d information. An ongoing area of research is the development of al g orithms that can continuously lear n from new information while retaining old information.

The future direct i ons of machine learning include several emerging areas. One such area is federated learning, which enables training models from distributed data sources while preserving data privacy. Blended l earning enables collaborative learning between different devices or educational institutions without sharing sensitive information, which preserves privacy and security.

Another exciting direction is the intersection of machine learning with other fields such as reinforcement learning and robotics. Reinforcement lea r ning involves training agents to make sequential decisions in an env i ronment to maximize rewards. By combining reinforcement learning and machine learning, researchers are trying to develop intelligent systems capable of making autonomous decisions in real-world scenarios.

In addition, there i s a growing interest in developing machine learning models that can handle uncertainty and make probabilistic predictions. Uncertainty assessment can help assess the reliability of model forecasts, allowing decision makers to make informed choices based on the level of uncertainty associated with the forecasts.

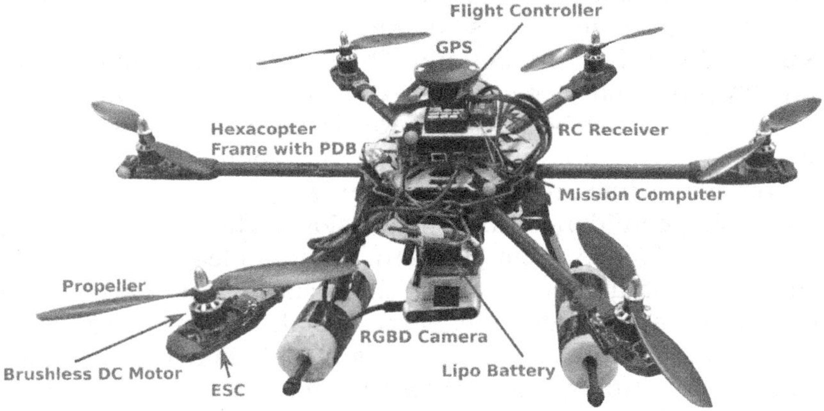

Autonomous Drone

Image depicts an autonomous drone, a prominent application of robotics and autonomous systems. Drones equipped with sensors, computer vision, and machine learning algorithms can perform tasks like aerial surveillance, package delivery, and even monitoring agricultural fields.

Machine learning-powered robotics and autonomous systems are revolutionising many different fields and sectors. Robots and autonomous systems can see, learn, and make wise decisions thanks to the incorporation of machine learning techniques, which has improved manufacturing, transportation, healthcare, and other industries. As academics in this interdisciplinary field continue to create cutting-edge algorithms and technologies, the future promises tremendous possibilities.

6.2. SENSOR FUSION AND PERCEPTION IN ROBOTICS

Robots' ability to detect and comprehend their surroundings depends heavily on sensor fusion and perception. It entails combining and processing input from numerous sensors to produce a cohesive and accurate picture of the robot's surroundings. As a result, the robot is able to decide for itself and carry out duties. Robot perception abilities are frequently improved using machine learning approaches.

Sensor Fusion

Sensor fusion in machine learning is a technique that combines information from multiple sensors to create a more accurate and reliable representation of the environment. Different types of sensors are used to capture different aspects of the world around us, including vision, lidar, radar, GPS, and more, in various applications such as autonomous vehicles, robotics, and augmented reality.

The process of sensor fusion involves integrating data from these different sensors to gain a more comprehensive understanding of the environment. By combining information from multiple sources, the system can overcome the limitations and uncertainties associated with individual sensors, improving perception and decision-making.

Sensor fusion techniques use different algorithms and models to combine and interpret data streams. These algorithms can include probabilistic filtering methods such as Kalman filters, particle filters, or advanced techniques such as Bayesian networks and deep learning architectures. The choice of algorithm depends on the characteristics of the sensors, the application area and the desired accuracy and real-time performance.

One common approach to sensor fusion is data alignment and calibration, which ensures that measurements from different sensors are synchronized and correctly scaled to a common coordinate system. This step is crucial to enable seamless integration of sensor data. Once the data is aligned, fusion algorithms can be used to combine and integrate the sensor values, taking into account their individual strengths and weaknesses. The benefits of sensor fusion are significant. By exploiting the complementary nature of various sensors, the system can improve its perception, improve target detection and tracking, enable robust positioning and mapping, and improve situational awareness. It also allows the system to handle ambiguous or conflicting sensor readings and make more informed decisions.

Sensor fusion algorithms can be classified into three main categories:

1. **Kalman Filtering:** Kalman filtering is a powerful mathematical technique used in machine learning and signal processing to estimate the state of a system by combining measurements and predictions. This is particularly effective in scenarios where

there are uncertainties in both the measurements and the dynamics of the underlying system. The algorithm is named after its creator, Rudolf E. Kalman.

At its core, Kalman filtering works as a recursive algorithm that iteratively updates the state estimate based on new measurements. It follows a two-step process: predict and update. In the prediction phase, the algorithm uses a system dynamic model to make a state prediction based on a previous estimate. This forecast includes all known control inputs that affect the system. The forecast also includes an assessment of the uncertainty associated with the country.

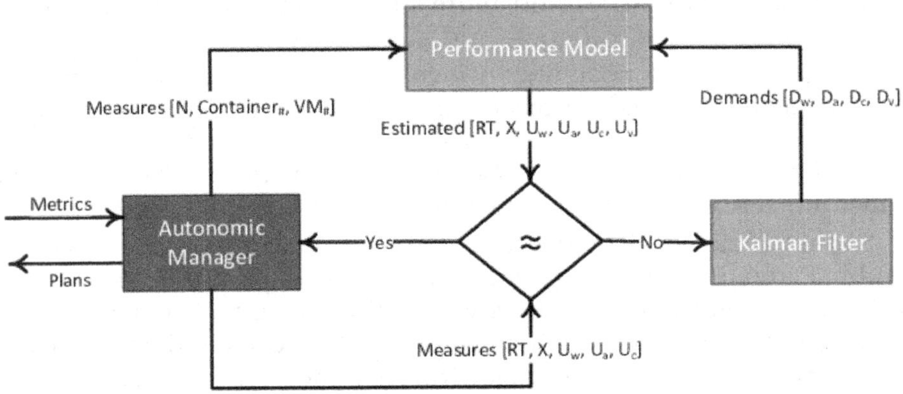

Kalman Filtering

Once the prediction is made, the algorithm moves to the update phase. At this point, the Kalman filter adds the last measurement to the estimation process. It compares the predicted state with the actual measurement, taking into account their respective uncertainties. The filter then adjusts the state estimate based on the measurement and updates the measurement uncertainty accordingly.

What distinguishes Kalman filtering from other estimation techniques is its ability to account for both process noise and measurement noise. Process noise refers to uncertainty in system dynamics, while measurement noise causes inaccuracies in sensor measurements. Considering these uncertainties, the Kalman filter provides a more reliable and accurate estimate of the system state.

Kalman Filtering finds many applications in machine learning, such as object tracking in computer vision, sensor fusion in autonomous vehicles, and localization in robotics. This is particularly valuable in scenarios where real-time state estimation is important and system dynamics and measurements are subject to noise and uncertainty.

2. Particle Filtering: Particle filtering, also known as sequential Monte Carlo (SMC) methods, is a powerful technique used in machine learning to estimate the hidden states of a dynamical system. This is particularly effective in scenarios where the system behaves in a non-linear and non-Gaussian manner.

Particle filtering is essentially a recursive Bayesian filtering algorithm that involves representing the posterior distribution of the hidden states of the system using a set of discrete particles. Each particle represents a hypothesis about the state at a given time and has a weight that reflects the probability that it is valid. These weights are updated as new observations occur, allowing the particles to dynamically track the true state of the system over time. The process starts with the first set of particles obtained from the prior distribution. Then, as new measurements are obtained, the particles are propagated further using a system dynamics model to predict the next state. These predictions are then adjusted or resampled based on the probability of measuring the predicted state. The sampling step assigns a higher weight to particles that better match the measurement results and discards particles that do not match the data well.

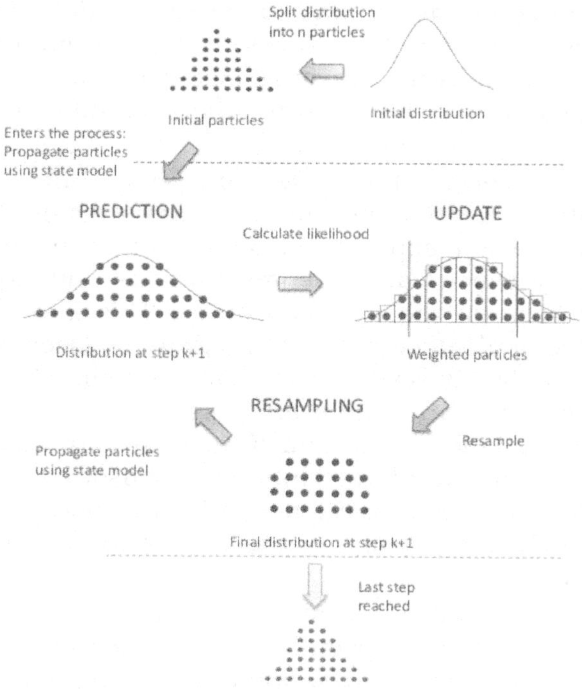

Particle Filtering

By repeatedly repeating the prediction and correction steps, particle filtering gradually refines the particle distribution by centering it around the true background state. A final estimate of the hidden space is usually obtained by summing the particle positions or calculating a statistic, such as the mean or mode of a set of particles.

Particle filtering is particularly useful in situations where the system has nonlinearities, non-Gaussian noise, and complex dependencies between variables. It has been successfully applied in many applications, including target tracking, simultaneous localization and mapping (SLAM), object tracking in computer vision, and system recognition.

However, particle filtration also has some limitations. As the number of particles increases, the computational complexity increases significantly. In addition, particle degeneracy can occur, where one particle dominates the entire particle population, causing a loss of diversity and an increase in estimation errors. Various techniques, such as resampling algorithms and particle diversity preservation strategies, have been proposed to address these challenges.

3. Deep Learning-based Fusion: Deep learning-based fusion is a machine learning technique that combines multiple data sources or features using deep neural networks. It aims to improve the overall performance of a machine learning model by effectively integrating different and complementary information from different categories or data streams.

Traditional fusion methods often use hand-crafted functions and simple algorithms to combine different data sources. However, deep learning-based fusion exploits the ability of deep neural networks to automatically learn feature representations and capture complex relationships between different categories. This approach allows for more advanced and efficient data integration. Deep learning-based fusion can be applied in several fields such as computer vision, natural language processing, and audio analysis. For example, in computer vision, it can combine visual data from images or videos with other categories, such as textual descriptions or sensor data. By combining these methods using deep neural networks, the model can leverage the strengths of each category and improve its overall understanding and predictive power.

One of the main advantages of deep learning-based fusion is its ability to handle heterogeneous data sources. It can seamlessly integrate different types of data, such as images, text, audio or time series data, into a coherent representation that captures underlying patterns and relationships. This allows the model to make more informed and accurate predictions.

In addition, deep learning-based fusion can learn complex feature interactions and dependencies between modalities that are often difficult to capture with traditional fusion techniques. Deep neural networks can automatically learn hierarchical representations that encode both low- and high-level semantic information about each category. This leads to a more complete and discriminative representation of the composite data, which improves the performance of various machine learning tasks.

Perception in Robotics

In robotics, perception plays a crucial role in machine learning because it enables robots to understand and interact with their environment. It involves acquiring, interpreting and using sensory information to make informed decisions and perform tasks effectively. Perception allows robots to perceive the world using various sensors such as cameras, lidar, radar and microphones, just as humans use their senses to perceive the environment.

In the context of machine learning, observation is often achieved using computer vision techniques. Computer vision algorithms process visual information collected by cameras or other image sensors to obtain meaningful information about the robot's environment. This information can include object recognition, detection, tracking and scene understanding. By analyzing visual data, robots can recognize objects, estimate their location and direction, and navigate complex environments.

Perception in robotics also extends beyond visual perception. Robots can also incorporate other sensory modalities such as depth sensors, touch sensors, and audio sensors to gather additional information about the environment. For example, depth sensors such as lidar provide depth information that allows robots to sense the distance to objects and create accurate 3D maps. Touch sensors allow robots to detect and respond to physical touch, allowing them to interact more effectively with objects and people. Audio sensors enable sound detection, allowing robots to recognize and interpret sound signals.

6.3. MAPPING AND LOCALIZATION

In the field of robotics and machine learning, localization and mapping are crucial tasks. Through the creation of maps and the determination of the robot's location within those maps, they involve the capacity to comprehend and navigate the environment.

Mapping

Machine learning mapping refers to the process of establishing a relationship between input data and corresponding output predictions or classifications. This is the basic concept behind various machine learning algorithms and models. The goal of mapping is to learn a function that can accurately predict or classify unseen data based on patterns and relationships observed in the training data.

In supervised learning, the more common mapping, a model is trained with labeled information, where each input is associated with a corresponding output or target value. The model learns to map input features to the desired output using different techniques, such as regression for continuous prediction or classification for discrete labeling. During mapping, model parameters are optimized through iterative processes such as gradient descent, minimizing the difference between predicted and actual results.

The complexity of the mapping can vary depending on the nature of the data and the problem to be solved. In simple cases, the mapping may involve direct relationships, such as linear regression, where the output is a linear combination of the input functions. However, in more complex scenarios, mapping may require non-linear relationships and interactions between features. Deep learning architectures such as neural networks are capable of learning complex mappings using multiple layers of interconnected neurons, allowing complex patterns and hierarchies to be captured in data. The quality of the mapping depends heavily on the availability and quality of the training data. With sufficient and rich data, the model can generalize well to unseen examples, while insufficient or biased data can lead to poor performance and limited applicability. Preprocessing techniques such as feature engineering and data augmentation can be used to enhance the mapping process by modifying or augmenting the input data to make it more suitable for learning.

Here's an example of a table illustrating a simple occupancy grid map representation:

X	Y	Occupancy
0	0	Free
1	0	Occupied
2	0	Free

X	Y	Occupancy
0	1	Free
1	1	Free
2	1	Occupied

Each grid cell's X and Y coordinates are shown in the table above, and the "Occupancy" column shows whether the cell is empty or occupied by an obstacle.

Localization

In machine learning, localization refers to the process of determining the location or location of objects or entities in an environment. It involves the use of various algorithms and techniques to accurately estimate the location of objects relative to a known coordinate system. Localization plays an important role in many applications, including autonomous vehicles, robotics, augmented reality and computer vision.

One of the main challenges in localization is handling uncertain and noisy sensor measurements. Most localization systems rely on sensor inputs such as GPS, cameras, lidar, radar or inertial measurement units (IMU). However, these sensors can cause errors and mistakes in the measurements, for example due to sensor noise, environmental conditions or blockage. Therefore, machine learning methods are often used to improve the accuracy and robustness of the localization process.

Machine learning techniques can be used to model the relationship between sensor measurements and the actual location of objects. It involves training a model using labeled data, where the inputs are the sensor measurements and the outputs are the corresponding ground truth stations. The trained model can then be used to predict the location of objects based on new sensor measurements. Common machine learning algorithms used for localization include regression models, support vector machines (SVM), random forests, or deep learning models such as convolutional neural networks (CNN) or recurrent neural networks (RNN).

Algorithms of localization can be divided into two main types: probability methods and geometric methods. Probabilistic methods, such as Kalman filters or particle filters, use statistical methods to estimate the position and the associated uncertainty. These methods consider system dynamics and combine data from multiple sensors to improve accuracy. Geometric methods, on the other hand, rely on geometric relationships between objects and sensors. These often involve techniques such as triangulation or feature matching to locate objects.

Recent advances in deep learning have greatly improved localization accuracy. For example, in computer vision applications, convolutional neural networks can learn to distinguish important features from images, enabling accurate object detection and localization. Similarly, recurrent neural networks can be used to process sequential sensor data such as IMU measurements and estimate the position of objects over time.

Overall, machine learning localization is an important area of research and development that enables machines to accurately understand and navigate their environment. Combining machine learning techniques with sensor fusion and probabilistic modeling has led to significant advances in localization, making it an essential part of many autonomous systems and smart applications.

Using probabilistic techniques, such as the Monte Carlo Localization (MCL) algorithm, is one popular way of localization. The MCL method uses a particle filter to maintain a set of particles, each of which represents a potential robot pose. on converge on the genuine pose, these particles are updated based on sensor measurements.

In numerous applications, such as autonomous cars, robotic exploration, and drone navigation, both mapping and localization play significant roles. Machines are capable of making wise decisions and navigating safely when they comprehend and portray the world appropriately.

6.4. MOTION PLANNING AND CONTROL

The development of algorithms and strategies for autonomous agents, such as robots or vehicles, to plan and carry out their actions in a dynamic and uncertain environment constitutes motion planning and control in machine learning. Numerous applications, such as autonomous vehicles, robotic manipulation, and unmanned aerial vehicles (UAVs), heavily rely on this sector.

Motion Planning

Motion design in machine learning refers to the process of designing algorithms and techniques that enable autonomous systems such as robots or self-driving vehicles to navigate and make decisions in complex and dynamic environments. It creates optimal or suboptimal paths or trajectories to reach a particular goal, taking into account various constraints and obstacles in the environment.

Machine learning plays a key role in motion planning because it provides the means to learn and adapt to the environment. For example, reinforcement learning allows agents to learn through interaction and feedback, allowing them to find optimal practices for motion planning tasks. By formulating the problem as a Markov Decision Process (MDP), the agent can learn to take actions that maximize cumulative benefits given the current state and possible future states. Another approach to machine learning motion planning is to use techniques such as supervised learning or deep learning to train models that can predict the outcome of various actions in a given environment. These models can be used to assess the feasibility and safety of possible paths or trajectories, allowing the agent to make informed decisions.

Machine learning motion planning also involves dealing with uncertainty and dynamic environments. Methods such as Monte Carlo Tree Search (MCTS) and Bayesian optimization can be used to study and evaluate various operations in uncertain environments. This allows the agent to adapt and update his plans based on new information or changing circumstances. In addition, motion design algorithms often incorporate computer vision and sensor integration techniques to perceive and understand the surrounding environment. Data from sensors such as cameras, lidar and radar can be used to create maps, detect obstacles and estimate the movement of other objects. These detection capabilities help create collision-free paths and avoid potential hazards.

Table 1: Motion Planning Algorithms

Algorithm	Description
Rapidly-Exploring Random Trees (RRT)	Incrementally builds a tree structure by randomly sampling the configuration space and expanding towards unexplored regions.
Probabilistic Roadmap (PRM)	Constructs a graph-based representation of the configuration space by sampling random configurations and connecting them to form a roadmap.
A* (A-Star)	Utilizes a search algorithm to find the optimal path by considering both the cost to reach a node and an estimated cost to the goal.
D* (D-Star)	Performs incremental search to find a path while considering dynamic changes in the environment.
Potential Fields	Uses artificial potential functions to guide the agent away from obstacles and towards the goal.
Dijkstra's Algorithm	Searches for the shortest path by considering the cost of traversing through nodes in a graph.

Motion Control

Motion control in machine learning refers to the application of computer algorithms and techniques that enable accurate and efficient control of physical movements in machines, robots or autonomous systems. This involves the integration of sensors, actuators and machine learning models to achieve accurate and adaptive motion control.

Machine learning algorithms play a key role in motion control because they allow the system to learn from data and make intelligent decisions based on observed patterns. These algorithms can be used to process sensor data such as vision, depth or inertial measurements and obtain relevant information about the current state of the environment and system. By analyzing this data, machine learning models can recognize patterns, predict future states, and make decisions about how to effectively control movement. One of the main areas where motion control machine learning finds applications is robotics. Robots often need to interact with their environment, perform tasks and move with precision and control. Machine learning techniques can be used to teach robots to autonomously learn and adapt their motion control strategies based on various factors such as object detection, obstacle avoidance, and task-specific requirements. By continuously monitoring and analyzing sensory data, the robot can adapt its movements to achieve optimal performance and improve control over time.

Motion control machine learning also plays an important role in other areas such as autonomous vehicles and industrial automation. In autonomous vehicles, machine learning algorithms can process data from various sensors such as cameras, LiDAR and radar and make decisions about steering, acceleration and braking. It enables the vehicle to navigate in difficult traffic situations and ensures safe and efficient traffic control.

Table 2: Motion Control Techniques

Technique	Description
Proportional-Integral-Derivative (PID) Control	Adjusts the control output based on the difference between the desired and actual state, taking into account the error, integral, and derivative terms.
Model Predictive Control (MPC)	Optimizes a finite-horizon control sequence by considering a model of the system and predicting its behavior over time.
Reinforcement Learning (RL)	Utilizes an agent that learns control policies through trial-and-error interactions with the environment, receiving rewards or penalties based on performance.

Trajectory Tracking Control	Regulates the agent's motion to follow a predefined trajectory by adjusting control signals, such as velocity or acceleration.
Adaptive Control	Adjusts control parameters in real-time to compensate for uncertainties or variations in the system's dynamics.
Sliding Mode Control	Applies discontinuous control actions to drive the system's state onto a predefined sliding surface and ensure robustness against disturbances or uncertainties.

6.5. REINFORCEMENT LEARNING FOR ROBOTICS

A branch of machine learning called reinforcement learning (RL) is concerned with creating methods and algorithms that allow agents to learn from their environment and make choices that would maximise a particular idea of cumulative reward. Because it enables robotic systems to learn autonomously and make decisions, RL has drawn a lot of interest in the field of robotics.

Reinforcement Learning Basics

Reinforcement learning (RL) is a subfield of machine learning that focuses on how an agent can learn to make decisions or act in an environment to maximize cumulative reward. It is inspired by the way humans and animals learn through trial and error and environmental feedback.

In RL, an agent interacts with the environment, which can be represented as a Markov Decision Process (MDP). The agent monitors the current state of the environment and acts based on a policy, which is a mapping from state to action. After performing an action, the agent receives feedback in the form of a reward signal that indicates the desirability of the agent's action in that state. The goal of the agent is to learn a policy that maximizes the expected cumulative reward over time.

In RL learning, the agent explores the environment and uses the information obtained in the search to make better decisions. Research is needed to discover new actions that can bring greater profits, while exploitation is about taking advantage of known actions that have already brought great rewards. Finding a balance between exploration and exploitation is a key challenge in RL.

One of the basic techniques in RL is called the Q-learning algorithm. Q-learning is a model-free RL method that learns an action value function, called the Q-function, that estimates the expected cumulative reward for performing a given action in a given state. The Q function is updated iteratively based on observed rewards and interactions of agents with the environment. By learning the Q function, the agent can choose actions that maximize its expected cumulative payoff.

RL Algorithms for Robotics

Reinforcement learning (RL) algorithms have received considerable attention and applications in robotics in the broader field of machine learning. RL provides a framework for teaching autonomous agents or robots to make sequential decisions while interacting with their environment. Unlike supervised learning, which relies on labeled data, and unsupervised learning, which looks for patterns in unlabeled data, RL focuses on trial-and-error learning.

In the context of robotics, RL algorithms allow robots to learn and improve their behavior by exploring their environment, receiving feedback, and optimizing their actions based on rewards or punishments. These algorithms typically involve an agent performing actions in the environment, monitoring the resulting state, and receiving feedback in the form of a reward signal. The agent's goal is to maximize cumulative benefits over time.

Different RL algorithms are used in robotics, each with its own strengths and perspectives. One commonly used algorithm is Q-learning, which is based on the concept of learning a function from operational values. Q-learning iteratively updates the Q-values of state-action pairs, allowing the robot to make informed decisions based on the estimated value of each action.

Another popular algorithm is Deep Q-Networks (DQN), which combines Q-learning with deep neural networks. DQN uses deep neural networks to approximate the action value function, enabling more complex and higher-dimensional spatial representations. This algorithm has been successful in several robotic applications, including autonomous navigation and manipulation tasks.

In addition, proximity policy optimization (PPO) is widely used in robotics due to its stability and efficiency. PPO directly optimizes policies by updating them in small steps, ensuring that the agent's behavior does not differ significantly from the previous policy. This stability is crucial in robotics, where safety and reliability are of the utmost importance. Other RL algorithms such as Actor-Critic, Trust Region Policy Optimization (TRPO) and Soft Actor-Critic (SAC) also find applications in robotics. These algorithms address a variety of challenges and considerations, including sampling efficiency, search-use tradeoffs, and continuous operations.

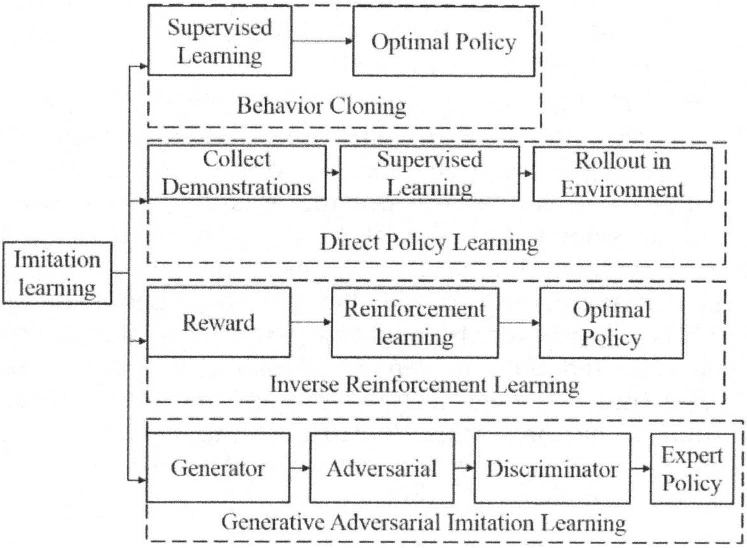

RL Algorithms for Robotics

6.6. ROBOT LEARNING FROM DEMONSTRATION

Robot Learning from Demonstration (LfD) is a branch of machine learning that aims to teach robots new skills or tasks through observation and imitation of human demonstrations. In LfD, the task is carried out by a human expert while the robot logs pertinent information such joint locations, velocities, and sensor readings. A machine learning algorithm is then trained using this data to mimic the shown behaviour.

Data Collection

Data collection is an important part of machine learning because it requires collecting and extracting relevant and high-quality data to train and develop accurate models. The data collection process involves the systematic acquisition of data points from various sources such as databases, APIs, sensor devices, social media platforms or human input. The collected data is the basis for training machine learning algorithms to identify patterns, make predictions or perform other tasks.

To ensure the effectiveness and reliability of machine learning models, several aspects must be considered in the data collection stage. First, it is important to define the problem description and define the specific information requirements that correspond to the desired result. This includes determining the type of data needed (eg, numerical, categorical, text, images, or audio) and defining appropriate attributes or identifiers for guided learning tasks.

Next, the methods and sources of data collection must be carefully selected. This may include designing studies, conducting experiments, collecting data from websites, using existing data, or establishing data collection pipelines. To avoid distortions and ensure generalizability, it is important to consider the representation and diversity of the data. Bias can arise from several sources, such as unbalanced data, biased samples, or systematic error in data collection processes. Data quality is another crucial factor in machine learning. It is important to validate and clean the collected data to remove outliers, missing values or incorrect entries that can negatively affect a model. Data processing techniques such as normalization, feature scaling, or dimensionality reduction can be used to improve data quality and suitability for specific machine learning algorithms.

Time (s)	Joint Angles (θ1, θ2, θ3, θ4, θ5, θ6)	End-Effector Position (x, y, z)
0.00	(0.25, 0.10, -0.15, 0.75, 1.00, 0.50)	(0.40, 0.60, 0.25)
0.10	(0.24, 0.12, -0.16, 0.73, 1.01, 0.49)	(0.39, 0.59, 0.26)
...	...	...
1.00	(0.22, 0.16, -0.19, 0.70, 1.03, 0.45)	(0.35, 0.55, 0.22)

Feature Extraction

Feature extraction is a crucial step in machine learning, where raw data is transformed into a form suitable for analysis by learning algorithms. Basically, it aims to identify and extract the most important information or features from data by reducing its size. This process is necessary to improve the effectiveness and efficiency of machine learning models.

The raw data used in machine learning often contains a large number of variables or attributes that may not all have an equal effect on the desired task. Some features may be noisy, redundant, or irrelevant, leading to suboptimal performance and increased computational complexity. Feature extraction solves this problem by selecting or creating a subset of features that best represent the underlying patterns or characteristics of the data.

There are several techniques for removing a feature, including both manual and automatic methods. Manual feature extraction involves domain knowledge and expertise to process appropriate features based on a specific problem domain. This approach can be effective when domain knowledge is rich and well understood, but it can be time-consuming and miss subtle connections in the data.

Feature removal plays an important role in improving model performance and generalization. By reducing the dimensionality of the data, it helps mitigate the curse of dimensionality, where the performance of machine learning algorithms degrades as the number of features increases. Additionally, feature extraction can reveal hidden relationships and patterns in data, making it easier to learn models and make accurate predictions

Time (s)	Joint Angles Feature Vector	End-Effector Position Feature Vector
0.00	(0.25, 0.10, -0.15, 0.75, 1.00, 0.50)	(0.40, 0.60, 0.25)
0.10	(0.24, 0.12, -0.16, 0.73, 1.01, 0.49)	(0.39, 0.59, 0.26)
...	...	...
1.00	(0.22, 0.16, -0.19, 0.70, 1.03, 0.45)	(0.35, 0.55, 0.22)

Learning Algorithm

In machine learning, a learning algorithm refers to a set of mathematical and computational techniques used to train a model to make predictions or decisions based on input data. It is an important part of machine learning and is responsible for extracting patterns, relationships and insights from data.

The learning algorithm works by iteratively adjusting the parameters of the mathematical model based on input-output pairs given in the training data. The goal is to minimize the difference between the model predictions and the actual values or items associated with the input data.

There are different types of learning algorithms, each suitable for different types of problems and data. Supervised learning algorithms learn from labeled examples where input data is matched with corresponding correct output labels. Their goal is to generalize from these examples to accurately predict the labels of new, previously unseen data. Examples of supervised learning algorithms include decision trees, support vector machines and neural networks.

On the other hand, unsupervised learning algorithms do not rely on labeled data. Instead, they try to find underlying patterns or structures in the data without prior knowledge of the labels of the results. Clustering algorithms such as k-means and hierarchical clustering are commonly used in unsupervised learning to group similar data points.

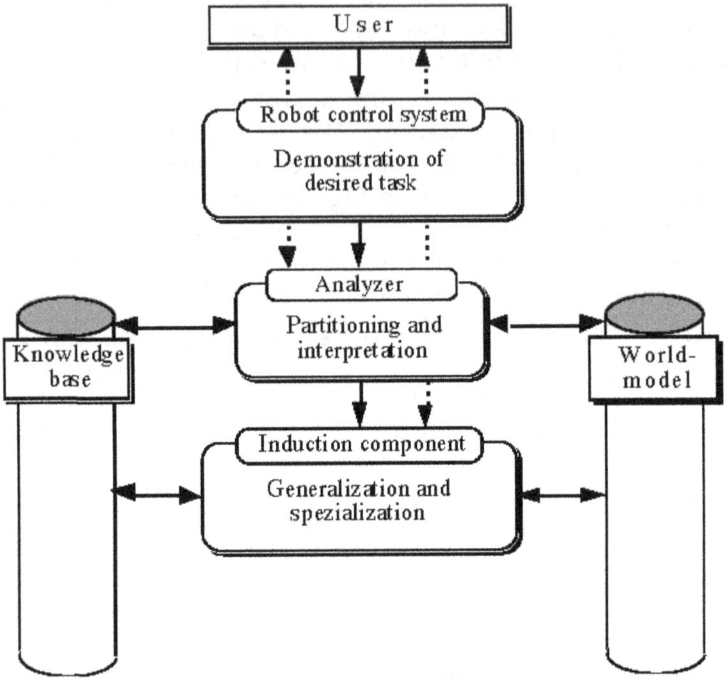

Robot Learning Algorithm

In addition, reinforcement learning algorithms focus on training agents to make optimal decisions in an environment. Agents learn through trial and error and receive feedback on their actions in the form of rewards or punishments. Over time, they learn to maximize their cumulative gains by exploring different strategies and using the most effective ones.

Learning algorithms can be further classified into batch learning and online learning. In ensemble learning, the model is trained on the entire dataset at once, which can be computationally expensive for large datasets. In contrast, online learning continuously updates the model as new information becomes available, allowing for more flexible and adaptive learning.

6.7. ROBOTICS AND AUTONOMOUS SYSTEMS IN THE FUTURE

Machine learning is heavily reliant on robotics and autonomous systems (RAS). As technology develops, robotics and machine learning are combined to create intelligent, autonomous systems that can do difficult tasks without the need for human interaction.

Applications of RAS in the Future

RAS (Robotics and Automation Systems) will play an important role in the future of machine learning. As machine learning algorithms advance, the integration of RAS technologies offers enormous opportunities to improve automation, efficiency and decision-making across industries. .

One of the applications of RAS in machine learning is in autonomous vehicles. Self-driving cars rely on machine learning algorithms to process massive amounts of data and make real-time decisions. RAS technologies such as sensors, actuators and intelligent control systems allow these vehicles to sense their surroundings, navigate complex road conditions and communicate with other vehicles and pedestrians. By combining machine learning with the RAS system, autonomous vehicles can continuously improve their performance, adapt to changing environments and increase traffic safety.

Another area where RAS has a significant impact on machine learning is industrial automation. By integrating machine learning algorithms into robotic systems, manufacturers can optimize production processes, improve quality control and reduce operating costs. RAS technology allows robots to perform complex tasks accurately and adaptively, while machine learning algorithms allow them to learn from data, recognize patterns and optimize their performance over time. This synergy between RAS and machine learning has the potential to revolutionize industries by enabling highly efficient and flexible production systems. In addition, RAS technology can be applied in healthcare, where machine learning algorithms are used for medical diagnosis, image recognition and personalized treatment. By combining RAS technologies such as robotic surgical systems and smart medical devices, healthcare providers can improve capacity, improve patient outcomes and improve efficiency. Machine learning algorithms can analyze vast amounts of medical data, aid in diagnosis and provide personalized treatment recommendations. RAS technology enables precise and minimally invasive procedures, which increases the accuracy and safety of medical procedures.

RAS has the potential to transform many different fields and industries. Here are a few crucial examples:

Application	Description
Manufacturing	Autonomous robots can handle repetitive tasks on assembly lines, increasing efficiency and productivity.
Healthcare	Robots can assist in surgeries, patient care, and rehabilitation, enhancing precision and reducing human error.

Application	Description
Agriculture	Autonomous drones and robots can be used for crop monitoring, irrigation, and harvesting, improving agricultural practices.
Transportation	Self-driving cars and delivery drones can enhance safety, reduce traffic congestion, and optimize logistics.
Service Industry	Robots can be employed in hotels, restaurants, and customer service, providing personalized experiences and assistance.
Exploration and Mining	Autonomous robots can explore uncharted territories and mines, enabling safer and more efficient resource extraction.

Components of RAS

RAS (Random Access Sampler) is an important component of machine learning, especially in the field of deep learning and neural networks. It plays a key role in the training process, effectively managing training data and providing access to it during the training phase.

The main purpose of RAS is to randomly select and sample a set of training data. This random sampling is important to ensure that the model learns from a range of examples and avoids biases or overfitting that may result from a sequential or deterministic selection process.

RAS is responsible for randomly shuffling the training data before each step or iteration of the training process. This shuffling helps reduce the model's dependence on the sequence of training examples and prevents it from memorizing or overfitting the training data.

Another important aspect of RAS is its ability to efficiently acquire and provide mini-data to the model during training. Instead of entering the entire data set at once, RAS divides the data into smaller subsets called minis. These mini-sets typically contain a fixed number of training examples and are drawn from a randomly shuffled dataset. This mini-ata approach enables more efficient computing and enables parallel processing on GPUs, which can significantly speed up the training process. RAS also ensures equal distribution of training data across classes or classes, especially in unbalanced datasets. This is achieved by techniques such as stratified sampling, where the random sampling process takes into account the class distribution of the data set.

Overall, RAS is an important component in machine learning because it helps build a more robust and generalizable model by providing rich and representative training data samples. By randomizing the data selection process and efficiently managing the mini-set, RAS contributes to the efficiency and effectiveness of the training process, leading to better model performance and improved learning outcomes.

7

Machine Learning in Cybersecurity

7.1. INTRODUCTION TO MACHINE LEARNING IN CYBERSECURITY

By enabling automated detection and reaction to constantly evolving threats, machine learning (ML) plays a significant role in cybersecurity. Massive amounts of data may be analysed by ML algorithms, which can also spot trends and forecast outcomes, improving the efficacy and efficiency of security measures.

Application Areas

Machine learning has emerged as a transformative technology with wide applications in various industries. The application areas of machine learning are diverse and rapidly expanding and disruptive industries such as healthcare, finance, e-commerce, transportation and many others.

In healthcare, machine learning is used to diagnose diseases, predict patient outcomes, and customize treatment plans. It analyzes vast amounts of medical data to identify patterns and make accurate predictions, helping doctors make informed decisions and improve patient care.

In the financial sector, machine learning plays a key role in fraud detection, credit scoring, algorithmic trading and risk management. It can analyze large financial data in real time, detect anomalies and identify potential risks, enabling financial institutions to make informed decisions and mitigate losses.

Online shopping platforms use machine learning algorithms to improve customer experience. Recommender systems analyze user preferences and behavior to provide personalized product recommendations, increasing customer satisfaction and increasing sales. In addition, machine learning is used for demand forecasting, inventory management and price optimization.

Transportation and logistics companies are using machine learning for route optimization, predictive maintenance, and autonomous vehicle development. By analyzing traffic patterns, weather conditions and historical data, machine learning algorithms can optimize delivery routes, reduce fuel consumption and improve the overall efficiency of the transport industry.

Key ML Techniques in Cybersecurity

Machine learning (ML) technologies play an important role in cyber security, providing advanced capabilities for threat detection, anomaly detection and risk assessment. These techniques use large volumes of data to train models that can effectively analyze and detect patterns in complex and dynamic cyber security environments.

One of the key technologies in cyber security is supervised learning. It contains data labeled using training models, where each data point is associated with a known class or outcome. This approach allows the model to learn from historical data and make predictions or classifications based on new, previously unseen data. In cybersecurity, supervised learning can be applied to, for example, malware detection, spam filtering, and intrusion detection, where a model learns to recognize malicious patterns based on known examples.

Another important cybersecurity ML technique is unsupervised learning. Unlike supervised learning, unsupervised learning is not based on labeled information. Instead, it focuses on identifying patterns and structures in data without prior knowledge of the results. This technique is particularly useful for anomaly detection, where the model can detect deviations from normal behavior and report possible threats or intrusions. Unsupervised learning algorithms, such as clustering and dimensionality reduction techniques, can help discover hidden relationships and anomalies in large data sets, aiding in network monitoring and detecting unusual patterns that may indicate malicious activity.

The following table summarizes some commonly used ML techniques in cybersecurity and their applications:

Technique	Description	Applications
Supervised Learning	Trains ML models using labeled data, enabling prediction or classification of new instances.	Malware detection, intrusion detection, phishing detection
Unsupervised Learning	Identifies patterns and anomalies in unlabeled data without prior knowledge.	Anomaly detection, network traffic analysis
Deep Learning	Utilizes artificial neural networks with multiple hidden layers for complex pattern recognition.	Image-based malware detection, malware classification
Reinforcement Learning	Uses an agent to learn from interactions with an environment to make optimal decisions.	Adaptive security systems, dynamic threat response

Benefits of ML in Cybersecurity

Machine learning (ML) offers a number of advantages in the field of cyber security, changing the way organizations detect, prevent and respond to cyber threats. ML algorithms have the ability to analyze vast amounts of data, identify patterns and make predictions, allowing security systems to become more predictive and effective. One of the main advantages of ML in cybersecurity is its ability to detect anomalies and identify previously unknown threats. ML models can learn common patterns of network traffic, user behavior, and system operations, allowing them to detect anomalies that may indicate malicious activity, such as intrusions or data breaches. By continuously learning and adapting, ML algorithms can improve their accuracy in distinguishing true threats from false positives, reducing the burden on security analysts and enabling faster response times. ML also plays a key role in automating threat detection and response processes. ML-enabled systems enable security teams to use real-time data analytics to quickly identify and prioritize potential threats. ML algorithms can analyze vast amounts of security logs, network traffic, and other related data sources to detect suspicious activity, malware, or malicious code. This automation enables faster incident response and improves the overall security of organizations by reducing the time between detection and resolution.

In addition, ML can help build robust predictive models for cyber risk assessment. By training ML algorithms on historical data from past cyber incidents, organizations can predict and quantify potential future risks. These predictive models help optimize resource allocation, prioritize security measures, and develop proactive strategies to mitigate threats. ML can also help manage vulnerability by identifying weaknesses in software systems or network infrastructure, allowing organizations to patch or fix vulnerabilities before they can be exploited.

7.2. INTRUSION PREVENTION AND DETECTION SYSTEMS

By detecting and stopping hostile activity, intrusion prevention and detection systems (IPDS) are essential for keeping computer networks secure. By enabling automatic and intelligent detection of network intrusions, machine learning techniques can improve IPDS's capabilities.

Intrusion Prevention and Detection Systems (IPDS):

Intrusion Prevention and Detection Systems (IPDS) play a key role in protecting computer networks and systems from malicious activity. These systems use machine learning techniques to detect and prevent unauthorized access, attacks and intrusions in real time.

IPDS uses a combination of signature-based and anomaly-based detection methods. Signature-based detection involves comparing network traffic or system activity against a database of known attack patterns or signatures. This approach is effective at detecting known threats such as viruses or malware, but may struggle to detect new or evolving attacks. To address this limitation, IPDS also uses anomaly detection. This method involves establishing a baseline of normal operation by analyzing network traffic, system logs, user behavior and other related data. Machine learning algorithms are then trained on that baseline to detect deviations from the norm. By continuously monitoring network activity, the system can report suspicious behavior that significantly deviates from established baselines.

Machine learning plays a crucial role in IPDS because it allows the system to adapt and learn new patterns and behaviors. As the system experiences new attacks or anomalies, it can add them to its database and improve its detection capabilities over time. Thanks to this adaptive learning, IPDS stays abreast of new threats, reducing the risk of false positives and false negatives.

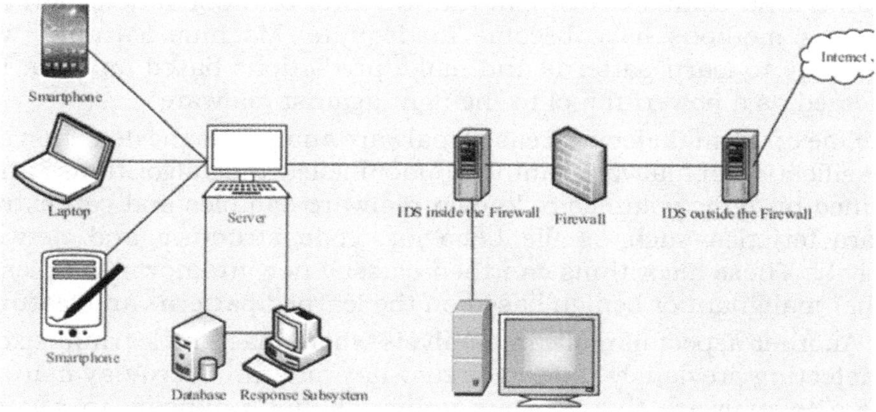

Intrusion Prevention and Detection Systems (IPDS)

IPDS also benefits from the scalability and processing power offered by machine learning. With a lot of network traffic and system logs to analyze, traditional rule-based systems can keep up. On the other hand, machine learning algorithms can efficiently process and analyze massive amounts of data, making IPDS more effective in real-time threat detection and prevention. In addition, IPDS can use machine learning techniques for advanced threat intelligence. By analyzing historical attack data and correlating it with external threat streams and security research, the system can identify patterns and signs of compromise that ordinary people might miss. This proactive approach improves the system's ability to detect and mitigate threats before they cause significant damage.

7.3. MALWARE ANALYSIS AND DETECTION

The analysis and detection of malware are essential components of computer security. Traditional signature-based detection techniques are frequently insufficient due to the complexity and sophistication of malware that is growing. The ability to analyse and detect malware has been improved with the use of machine learning techniques.

Malware Analysis

Malware analysis in machine learning involves the application of advanced techniques and algorithms to detect, classify and understand malware (commonly known as malware). Due to the ever-increasing number and complexity of malware threats, traditional detection and analysis methods have become inadequate. Machine learning, with its ability to learn patterns and make predictions based on data, has emerged as a powerful tool in the fight against malware.

One of the main focus areas of malware analysis is the detection and classification of malware samples. Machine learning algorithms can be trained on large volumes of known malware samples and can extract characteristics such as file behavior, code structure and network activity. These algorithms can then classify new unknown samples as either malignant or benign based on the learned patterns and features.

Another aspect of malware analysis where machine learning excels is detecting previously unseen or zero-day malware. Zero-day malware refers to malware that exploits vulnerabilities unknown to security experts. Machine learning algorithms can analyze system behavior and network traffic, detect anomalies, and detect suspicious patterns that may indicate the presence of zero-day malware.

Machine Learning in Malware Detection

Machine learning has become a powerful tool in malware detection, revolutionizing the way security professionals combat evolving cyber threats. Malware or malicious software refers to any number of programs designed to disrupt, damage, or gain unauthorized access to computer systems. Traditional signature-based detection methods, which rely on predetermined patterns to identify known malware, cannot keep up with the rapidly evolving nature of cyber threats.

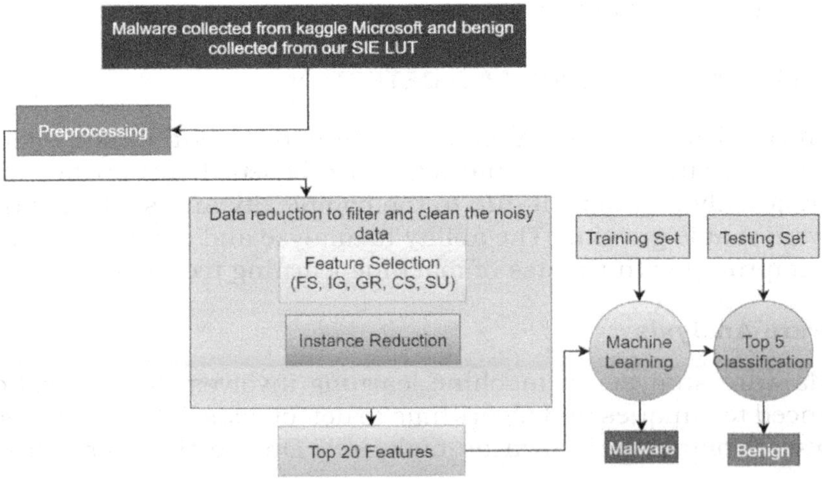

Machine Learning in Malware Detection

Machine learning algorithms, on the other hand, offer a dynamic and adaptive approach to malware detection. These algorithms can be trained on large datasets containing both benign and malicious samples, allowing them to learn the complex patterns and characteristics of different types of malware. Machine learning models can extract relevant information and identify potential threats by analyzing various characteristics such as file attributes, network traffic, system behavior and code structure.

One of the main advantages of machine learning in malware detection is its ability to detect previously unseen or zero-day attacks. Zero-day attacks refer to vulnerabilities that are unknown to security experts and for which there are no patches or signatures. Machine learning models can detect anomalies and deviations from normal behavior, allowing them to flag potentially malicious activity even if it doesn't match known malware signatures.

Malware detection uses a variety of machine learning techniques, including supervised learning, unsupervised learning, and deep learning. Supervised learning involves training models that use labeled data sets, where each sample is classified as benign or malignant. In contrast, unsupervised learning does not rely on predefined labels, but instead detects patterns and anomalies in the data. Deep learning, a subset of machine learning, uses multi-layer neural networks to extract complex features and make highly accurate predictions.

Feature engineering plays a critical role in building effective machine learning models for malware detection. Security experts must carefully select and design features that capture the characteristics of malware. These characteristics may include file size, file format, API calls, system calls, and network traffic patterns. In addition, advanced techniques such as dynamic analysis, sandboxing and behavioral analysis are often combined with machine learning to improve the accuracy and efficiency of malware detection systems.

Although machine learning has greatly improved malware detection, it is not without problems. Malicious attacks, where malware authors try to avoid detection by manipulating or obfuscating their code, pose a serious threat. Furthermore, ensuring the scalability and effectiveness of machine learning models in real-time detection scenarios is still an ongoing area of research.

Network Traffic Analysis

Network traffic a n alysis in machine learning involves the application of ad v anced algorithms and techniques to analyze and interpret pattern s, behaviors and anomalies in network traffic data.

As the volume and complexity of network traffic increases, traditional methods for monitor i ng and analyzing network data have become inadequate. Machine learning techniques offer a promising solution to gain valuable insights and identify potential threats or vulnerabilities.

Machine learning models can be trained on large datasets of web traffic to learn common patterns and behaviors of online communication. These patterns can then be used to detect deviations from normal behavior, such as network intrusions, malicious activity or unusual traffic patterns. By continuously monitoring network traffic and using machine learning algorithms, organizations can improve their ability to detect and respond to security breaches in real time.

There are different approaches to analyze network traffic using machine learning. One common method is to use supervised learning, where using identif i ed training data, a model is trained to classify network traffic into different categories, such as normal or malicious. Unsupervised learni n g techniques such as clustering or anomaly detection can also be used to detect patterns or anomalies in network traffic data without the need for predefined identifiers.

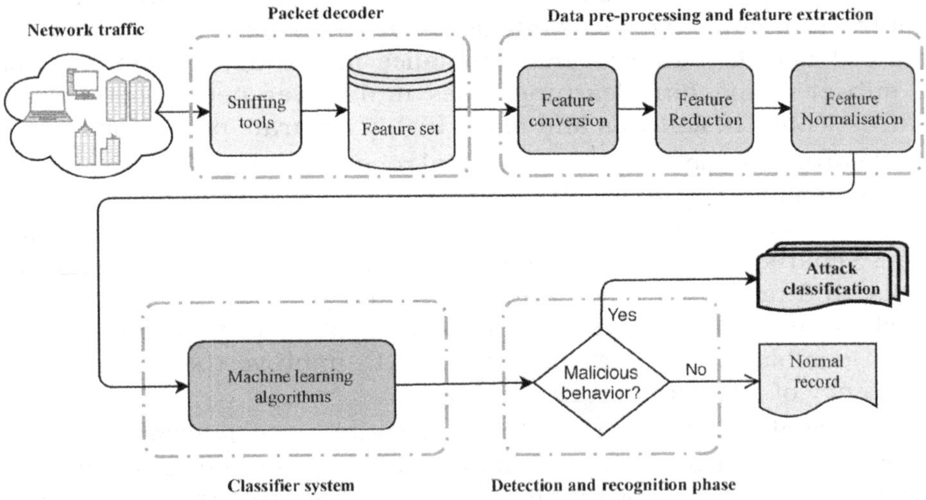

Network Traffic Analysis

Feature extraction is an important step in web traffic analysis. Machine learning algorithms need relevant features to learn and make predictions effectively. Attributes can include packet-level information such as packet size, protocol type, or source and destination IP addresses, as well as higher-level attributes such as traffic volume, flow duration, or payload content. The selection and design of appropriate features significantly affects the performance and accuracy of machine learning models.

Network traffic analysis in machine learning is not limited to information security applications. It can also be used for network performance optimization, capacity planning and traffic management. By analyzing network traffic patterns, organizations can identify bottlenecks, predict congestion and optimize network resources to ensure smooth and efficient operations.

However, analyzing network traffic in machine learning is not without problems. The large volume and speed of Internet data requires scalable and efficient algorithms that can process and analyze the data in real time. The implementation of effective network traffic analysis systems is also challenged by data protection issues and the need to handle sensitive data.

In summary, machine learning from network traffic analysis provides an effective approach to monitor, detect and respond to network security threats and optimize network performance. By leveraging machine learning algorithms, organizations can gain deeper insights into their network traffic, improve their cybersecurity, and improve overall network performance.

Let's look at a table that shows the many kinds of anomalies that network traffic analysis can identify:

Anomaly Type	Description
Port Scanning	Unusual scanning activities targeting multiple ports
Denial of Service	Intentional attempts to disrupt or overload a network or service
Data Exfiltration	Unauthorized transfer of sensitive data from a network
Malware Traffic	Suspicious network activities associated with malware
DNS Tunneling	Illegitimate use of DNS protocol for unauthorized data transfer

The network flows are visualised in this graphic by a line linking each flow's source IP address to its destination IP address. In order to detect abnormalities or patterns in the network traffic, the lines' thickness or colour can be used to depict the amount of traffic flowing between the endpoints.

7.4. SECURITY EVENT CLASSIFICATION AND LOG ANALYSIS

An important area of cybersecurity is Security Event Classification and Log Analysis, which uses machine learning algorithms to classify security events and examine log data to look for potential risks. In order to identify trends and abnormalities in log files, machine learning algorithms are trained on labelled datasets. This process enables the system to forecast the future and take the necessary action.

Security Event Classification

Security incident classification in machine learning refers to the classification and labeling of security-related incidents or incidents using advanced data processing techniques. As security threats and attacks increase in number and complexity in today's digital environment, automated classification systems have become essential for effective incident response and proactive security measures.

Machine learning algorithms are trained for various security incidents involving various cyber threats, vulnerabilities and anomalies. These algorithms learn patterns, relationships and characteristics in the data to distinguish between different categories of security events.

The classification process usually involves data processing, significant feature extraction, and an appropriate machine learning algorithm. Feature extraction techniques may include analyzing network traffic, system logs, user behavior, or other relevant indicators to gather meaningful information about security events. The selected machine learning algorithm is then trained using labeled data, where human experts have classified security events into different categories.

Once a classification model is trained, it can be deployed in real-time systems to automatically classify incoming security events. The model takes the extracted features as input and predicts the class or category to which the event belongs. This may include identifying events such as malware infection, network intrusion, data breach, phishing attempt or other predefined categories. Machine learning has several advantages in classifying information security events. It enables organizations to automate the initial classification and prioritization of security incidents, enabling faster response times and reducing the workload of security analysts. It also improves threat detection by identifying patterns and anomalies that may not be obvious to human users. In addition, machine learning models can adapt and evolve over time, constantly learning from new data, making them more effective in dealing with new and evolving security threats.

Tables can be used to display how security incidents are categorised. Here is a sample table showing various security event classes:

Class	Description
Malware	Events related to the presence or execution of malware
Intrusion	Unauthorized access or attempts to breach the system
Denial of Service	Deliberate actions to disrupt the system or network
Data Breach	Unauthorized access or disclosure of sensitive data
Phishing	Attempts to deceive users and acquire sensitive information

Log Analysis

Log analysis in machine learning refers to the process of extracting valuable insights and patterns from log data generated by various systems, applications, or devices. Logs contain a wealth of information about system operation and behavior, making them a valuable resource for troubleshooting, performance optimization, and security analysis. By applying machine learning techniques to record analysis, it is possible to automate anomaly detection, identify behavioral patterns and predict future events.

Log analytics uses machine learning algorithms to process and analyze large amounts of log data that can be difficult to process manually due to its sheer volume and complexity. These algorithms learn from historical log data and are trained to identify patterns, trends, and anomalies that may indicate specific events or problems. They can automatically detect common patterns, such as errors, warnings, or performance bottlenecks, and report anomalies that differ from expected behavior.

One of the main advantages of using machine learning in log analysis is its ability to handle the dynamic nature of log data. As systems evolve and new patterns emerge, machine learning models can adapt and update their understanding of normal and abnormal behavior. This configurability enables proactive monitoring and early detection of potential problems, reducing the time and effort required for manual analysis and troubleshooting.

Additionally, machine learning can help correlate logs from multiple sources. By integrating information from different protocols and systems, it is possible to obtain a complete picture of the functionality of the entire system and identify complex interactions and dependencies. For example, machine learning algorithms can identify patterns that indicate a sequence of events leading to a critical failure, or identify potential security breaches by analyzing log data from various sources.

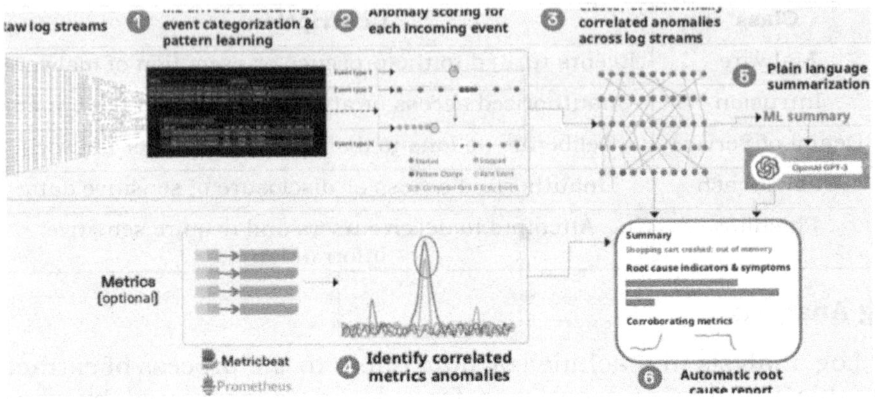

Log Analysis

Machine Learning in Security Event Classification and Log Analysis

Machine learning plays a key role in security event classification and log analysis, revolutionizing how organizations identify and respond to potential threats. In the context of security, various systems, devices, and applications create logs that store information about user activity, network traffic, system events, and more. These logs contain a lot of information that can be overwhelming to analyze manually, making it difficult to identify and prioritize vulnerabilities in real time.

Machine learning techniques enable automatic analysis and classification of security events and logs, providing a scalable and efficient solution to this problem. By training models on historical data, machine learning algorithms can learn patterns and correlations that indicate certain types of security events or abnormal behavior. This enables them to accurately categorize and classify upcoming events or logs and flag potential threats for further investigation.

Incident classification involves tagging security events based on their characteristics, such as severity, type, or system impact. Machine learning models can be trained to detect different categories of security events, such as malware infections, unauthorized access attempts, or suspicious network activity. These models can learn from labeled examples and then generalize their knowledge to classify new unseen events.

Log analysis, on the other hand, focuses on gaining meaningful insights from logs to identify information security problems or anomalies. Machine learning algorithms can be used to analyze log patterns and detect deviations from normal behavior. For example, they can detect unusual login patterns, unexpected system changes, or unusual network traffic that may indicate a potential security breach.

Tables can be used to display the trained model's performance metrics when contrasting various techniques or model iterations. Here is an illustration table comparing the F1 score and accuracy of various machine learning algorithms:

Algorithm	Accuracy (%)	F1 Score
Decision Tree	92	0.91
Random Forest	94	0.93
Neural Network	96	0.95

To summarise, machine learning techniques are used in security event classification and log analysis to automatically classify security events and examine log data. Images can be used to visualise the findings of log analysis or patterns in log data over time, whereas tables can be used to illustrate the classification of security events or performance metrics of machine learning algorithms. These visual aids assist in more easily comprehending and analysing the results.

7.5 DEFENSE TECHNIQUES AND ADVERSARIAL MACHINE LEARNING

Defense Techniques in Machine Learning

Machine learning defense techniques refer to a set of strategies and methods used to protect machine learning models against adversarial attacks, data poisoning, or other forms of malicious exploitation. As machine learning models become more common in many different fields, it is important to ensure their robustness and reliability. Defense techniques aim to reduce the vulnerability of these models and improve their resilience.

One widely used defense technique is adversarial training, which involves training machine learning models on both pure and adversarial examples. By showing the models to a carefully designed opponent during training, they can learn to generalize and better identify potential threats. Responsive training introduces a form of regularity that helps models resist robustness attacks.

Another protection method is input sanitization, which involves preprocessing or filtering input data to identify and remove potentially malicious input or anomalies. This technique can help identify and reject inputs that may be specifically designed to deceive or manipulate the model. Input cleaning methods can range from simple data normalization to more complex anomaly detection algorithms.

Machine learning also uses ensemble methods for protection. Ensemble models combine forecasts from several individual models to improve overall accuracy and reliability. By aggregating predictions from different models trained with different techniques or different subsets of data, complex methods can effectively reduce the impact of competing attacks and improve generality.

In addition, model introspection techniques are used to understand and identify behavioral anomalies in machine learning models. These methods include monitoring model output, examining decision limits, or analyzing factors in the model to detect suspicious activity or deviations from expected behavior. Model introspection can provide insight into potential vulnerabilities or signs of enemy attacks. In addition, regularization techniques such as termination, weighting or early termination are often used to avoid overfitting and improve generalization in machine learning models. By reducing the model's sensitivity to small changes in the input data, regularization methods can indirectly improve its resistance to adversarial attacks.

Adversarial Machine Learning

Adverbial machine learning is a subfield of machine learning that focuses on studying and defending against attacks against machine learning models. In traditional machine learning, models are trained and deployed on the assumption that the data they encounter during deployment is similar to the data used in training. However, adversarial attacks exploit vulnerabilities in machine learning models by introducing carefully crafted inputs designed to trick or deceive the model.

One common type of counterattack is the perturbation attack, in which small, imperceptible changes are made to the input data to mislead the model's predictions. These disturbances can be carefully created using techniques such as the Fast Gradient Sign Method (FGSM) or more sophisticated methods such as Projected Gradient Calculation (PGD). These attacks aim to exploit the sensitivity of the model to these disturbances and make it make false predictions.

The goal of adversarial machine learning researchers is to develop robust models that can withstand such attacks. Techniques such as adversarial training are used, where the model is trained with both pure and adversarial examples to improve its robustness. Responsive training involves generating competing examples during the training process and augmenting the training data with these examples to expose the model to a wide range of possible attacks.

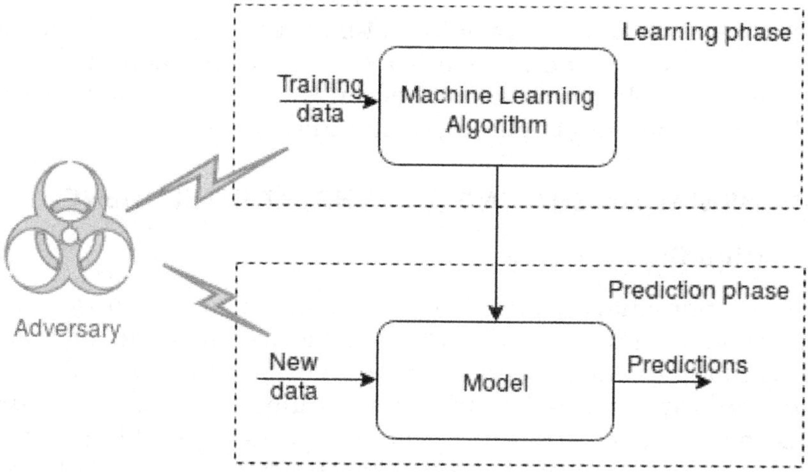

Adversarial Machine Learning

Another approach is to use detection and defense mechanisms to detect and mitigate counterattacks. These mechanisms may include extraordinary detection techniques, statistical analysis, or the use of specialized models that specifically focus on identifying competing inputs. In addition, techniques such as input sanitation or authentication can be used to ensure that input data conforms to expected patterns and reduce the risk of adversarial attacks.

Competitive machine learning is a rapidly evolving field with constant research and development. As new attack methods are developed, researchers continue to explore innovative defense strategies to improve the robustness and security of machine learning models. The goal is to create models that not only achieve high accuracy, but also demonstrate resistance to adversarial attacks, ensuring their reliability and trustworthiness in real applications.

An example table demonstrating different defence strategies and their attributes is provided below:

Defense Technique	**Description**
Adversarial Training	Model trained on adversarial examples
Defensive Distillation	Model predicts softened probabilities of another model
Feature Squeezing	Apply transformations to reduce search space
Ensemble Methods	Combine predictions of multiple models
Gradient Masking	Obfuscate sensitive information in gradients

7.6. PRIVACY-PRESERVING MACHINE LEARNING FOR SECURITY

Developing methods and algorithms to safeguard the privacy of sensitive data while carrying out machine learning tasks is the focus of the subject of study known as privacy-preserving machine learning. It attempts to establish a balance between the necessity of data analysis and the protection of people's personal information.

7.7. INFORMATION SHARING AND THREAT INTELLIGENCE

Information Sharing

Information sharing and threat intelligence are important in cyber security and machine learning. They enable organizations to proactively identify, mitigate and respond to potential threats, vulnerabilities and attacks. In this context, machine learning techniques are used to analyze and understand huge amounts of data, making it easier to identify patterns, anomalies and potential risks. This article explores the relationship between information sharing, threat intelligence and machine learning and the benefits they offer in the cyber security environment. Information sharing involves the exchange of knowledge, insights, and information between different entities, such as organizations, industries, and even governments, to collectively improve their situational awareness and defense against cyber threats. Information can be shared through various channels, including official platforms, industry associations and trusted networks. The main goal is to create a collaborative environment where organizations can improve their information security together.

Benefits of Information Sharing

Information sharing plays a vital role in advancing machine learning and its applications. By sharing information, data scientists and researchers can pool their resources, knowledge and experience, which leads to several important benefits. First, sharing information promotes collaboration and collective learning. When experts from different backgrounds come together to share their findings, methods and knowledge, they can work together to solve complex problems and develop more effective solutions. Such a collaborative approach not only improves the quality of research, but also accelerates the pace of innovation in the field of machine learning. Second, information sharing promotes reproducibility and transparency. By publicly sharing data sets, algorithms, and experimental methods, researchers allow others to verify and replicate their results. This transparency strengthens the scientific integrity of machine learning research and increases trust in the community. This can be used to identify potential biases or shortcomings in models, leading to improvements and advances in the field.

Finally, sharing encourages interdisciplinary collaboration. Machine learning has applications in several fields such as healthcare, finance and transportation. By sharing information, experts from different fields can collaborate, combining their domain-specific expertise with machine learning expertise. This multidisciplinary approach leads to the development of innovative solutions that address complex challenges and have a real impact.

Threat Intelligence

Machine learning threat intelligence refers to the application of advanced analytics and algorithms to identify, analyze and predict potential threats and attacks in the cyber security industry. This involves collecting and analyzing large amounts of data from various sources such as internet logs, malware samples, social media and dark web forums to proactively identify and mitigate security risks.

Machine learning algorithms play a key role in threat intelligence as they automatically process and analyze large data sets to discover patterns, anomalies and indicators of compromise. These algorithms learn from historical data and constantly adapt to new information, enabling the detection of new threats and the prediction of future attack vectors.

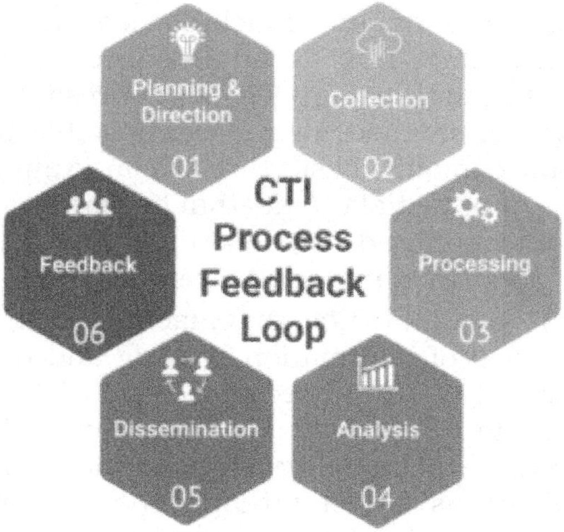

CTI feedback Loop

One of the main advantages of using machine learning in threat intelligence is its ability to detect previously unknown or zero-day attacks. Traditional rules-based systems often struggle to keep up with the rapidly evolving threat landscape because they rely on predefined rules and signatures. In contrast, machine learning models can detect unknown threats by identifying anomalies in data patterns, behaviors or characteristics that deviate from normal operation.

Another area where machine learning excels in threat intelligence is automated threat hunting. By analyzing large volumes of data in real time, machine learning algorithms can identify potential threats that human analysts might miss. This enables security teams to proactively respond to threats, reduce response time and prevent potential data breaches. In addition, machine learning techniques can be applied to enrich threat intelligence. By integrating external data sources such as threat streams, vulnerability databases and threat actor profiles, machine learning models can provide contextual intelligence and improve the accuracy and relevance of threat analysis.

Machine Learning in Information Sharing and Threat Intelligence

Machine learning has revolutionized the field of information sharing and threat intelligence, enabling more efficient and effective analysis of massive amounts of data. As the number and complexity of cyber security threats increase, traditional manual methods of data analysis and pattern recognition are insufficient. On the other hand, machine learning algorithms have the ability to automatically learn and adapt to data, making them invaluable tools in the fight against cyber threats.

When sharing information, machine learning algorithms can analyze and classify data from multiple sources, including network logs, security events and threat intelligence sources, to identify patterns and indicators of compromise. By automating this process, machine learning algorithms can quickly sift through large amounts of data and identify anomalies or potential threats that human analysts might miss. This speeds up detection and response time to new threats, enabling organizations to proactively protect their systems and networks.

However, it is important to note that machine learning is not without challenges in the field of information sharing and threat intelligence. The quality and variety of data used to train machine learning models has a significant impact on their performance. Furthermore, the interpretability and explainability of machine learning algorithms remains a concern, as understanding the reasons behind their decisions is crucial in the context of cyber security.

In conclusion, machine learning plays an important role in sharing information and threat intelligence by automating data analysis, improving threat detection and enabling collaboration between organizations. Although there are challenges to be overcome, the integration of machine learning in this field has enormous potential to strengthen cybersecurity in the face of ever-evolving threats.

7.8. FUTURE DIRECTIONS IN CYBERSECURITY: MACHINE LEARNING

Future Directions in Machine Learning for Cybersecurity

1. Adversarial Machine Learning: Adverbial machine learning is a branch of machine learning that focuses on understanding and defending against peer-to-peer attacks. A liability attack is a deliberate attempt to manipulate or deceive a machine learning model by exploiting its vulnerabilities. These attacks are aimed at tricking the model into making incorrect predictions or misclassifying the data.

One common type of counterattack is the perturbation attack, where imperceptible changes are made to the input data to fool the model. For example, adding small, carefully crafted perturbations to an image can cause an image classification model to completely misclassify it. To protect against such attacks, competing machine learning researchers are developing techniques that increase the robustness and security of machine learning models. This involves developing adversarial training methods, where models are trained on both clean and adversarial examples to learn to be more resistant to attacks. Competing training involves generating competing examples during the training process and incorporating them into the training dataset, forcing the model to learn from them and improve its ability to handle competing inputs.

Another way to protect against competitive attacks is to use detection and defense mechanisms. The purpose of these mechanisms is to identify and mark conflicting examples either in the inference phase or as input to the model. They use techniques such as anomaly detection, statistical analysis, or rule-based methods to identify likely conflicting inputs and take appropriate actions.

2. Privacy-Preserving Machine Learning: Privacy-preserving machine learning is a rapidly growing field that focuses on developing techniques to protect sensitive data by enabling the training and inference of machine learning models. Traditional machine learning algorithms often require access to large amounts of raw data, including personal data, raising privacy concerns and potential risks of data breaches or misuse.

Privacy-preserving machine learning attempts to solve these problems by using various cryptographic and privacy-enhancing techniques. One widely used approach is secure multiparty computing (MPC), which allows multiple parties to jointly train a model on their private datasets without sharing the data itself. MPC ensures that no party can access the other's information and the presentation of the final model is comparable to that achieved by traditional methods. Another frequently used technique is homomorphic encryption, which allows the encrypted data to be computed without actually encrypting it. With homomorphic encryption, the data remains encrypted throughout the training process, allowing multiple parties to perform computations on the encrypted data together while maintaining privacy. This approach ensures that sensitive information is never disclosed to any party involved in model training.

Differential privacy is another important concept in privacy-preserving machine learning. It provides a mathematical framework for quantifying and managing privacy risks associated with data analysis. By adding carefully calibrated noise to the training data or model parameters, differential privacy prevents leakage of individual information during the learning process. This provides a level of privacy protection while maintaining reasonable accuracy of model predictions.

Federated learning is an emerging approach that addresses privacy concerns using distributed data source learning models. In cooperative learning, models are trained on external devices (such as smartphones) or on local servers that store data, thus ensuring that the data remains on the devices and is not transferred to a central server. Only model updates bundled from multiple devices are shared, preserving individual data. Privacy-preserving machine learning techniques offer a promising way to reconcile the need for data protection with the growing demand for data solutions. By enabling secure collaboration and protecting sensitive data, these technologies facilitate the development of machine learning models while ensuring that individuals' privacy is protected. As the industry continues to evolve, it has the potential to revolutionize a number of industries, including healthcare, finance and other sensitive industries where privacy is paramount.

3. Secure and Trusted Machine Learning: Secure and reliable machine learning is an important part of ensuring the integrity, confidentiality and reliability of machine learning models and systems. As machine learning plays an increasingly important role in fields such as healthcare, finance and autonomous vehicles, the need for robust security measures becomes paramount.

One of the most important challenges for secure and reliable machine learning is protecting the confidentiality of sensitive data used in model training. This requires the adoption of technologies such as secure multi-party computing, discrete privacy and blended learning to prevent unauthorized access to raw data. By encrypting data during transmission and training, these methods enable collaboration and model development without compromising privacy. Another aspect of secure machine learning is ensuring the integrity of the models throughout their lifetime. Accountability attacks, where malicious actors manipulate or corrupt data to deceive models, pose a significant risk. Techniques such as adversarial training, model robustness checking and anomaly detection can help detect and mitigate these attacks, making models more reliable.

In addition, the interpretability and transparency of the models are crucial for building trust in machine learning systems. Interpretable models allow users to understand the underlying decision-making process and detect bias or discrimination. Techniques such as rule-based models, feature importance analysis and explanatory AI techniques help understand how models arrive at their predictions, enabling human oversight and accountability.

In addition, secure deployment and runtime monitoring are essential for the continued reliability of machine learning systems. Secure deployment involves protecting models from unauthorized access or tampering, while runtime monitoring detects anomalies or changes in model behavior that may indicate attacks or data drift. Technologies such as model watermarking, protected enclaves and anomaly detection algorithms are very important in maintaining the security and reliability of the models in use.

In short, secure and reliable machine learning focuses on ensuring the confidentiality, integrity and transparency of machine learning models and systems. By leveraging robust technologies throughout the lifecycle from data collection to deployment, organizations can reduce risk, protect sensitive data, and build trust in the reliability and fairness of machine learning applications.

4. Threat Intelligence and Analytics: Machine learning from threat intelligence and analytics is a powerful combination to improve the cybersecurity landscape. A threat intelligence system refers to the collection, analysis, and interpretation of information about potential and existing threats to an organization's information systems. This includes gathering information from various sources such as security vendors, open source intelligence, dark web monitoring and internal security logs.

Machine learning, on the other hand, is a branch of artificial intelligence that allows systems to automatically learn and improve from experience without being specifically programmed. This involves developing algorithms and models that can analyze data, identify patterns and make predictions or decisions. When machine learning algorithms are applied to threat intelligence, they can significantly improve the ability to detect, predict and respond to security threats. By processing vast amounts of data, including real-time security logs, network traffic and threat streams, machine learning models can identify anomalies, patterns of malicious behavior and signs of compromise.

Machine learning algorithms can also help automate the analysis of threat intelligence, reducing the manual work required to identify and prioritize potential threats. They can categorize and group data, extract relevant characteristics and generate actionable insights that help security teams respond effectively to emerging threats.

Additionally, machine learning can help develop predictive models that predict future threats based on historical data and ongoing trends. By identifying patterns and correlations, these models can provide early warnings and support proactive measures to reduce risks before they materialize.

However, it is important to note that machine learning threat intelligence and analysis is not without problems. The quality and relevance of the data used to train machine learning models are critical factors that can greatly affect their effectiveness. Data protection and security aspects must also be considered, as threat intelligence often contains sensitive information.

In short, it can be stated that the integration of threat intelligence and analysis with machine learning offers excellent opportunities for strengthening cyber security. By using advanced algorithms and data analysis techniques, organizations can gain more insight into potential threats, improve their threat detection capabilities, and proactively protect their information systems against evolving cyber threats.

8

Machine Learning Emerging Trends and Future Directions

8.1 EXPLAINABLE AI

Explanatory artificial intelligence, also known as interpretable artificial intelligence or transparent artificial intelligence, is an area of machine learning research that focuses on developing models and algorithms that can provide understandable explanations for their decisions and predictions. Although traditional machine learning models such as deep neural networks have shown impressive performance in various fields, their inner workings are often considered black boxes, making it difficult for people to understand why a certain decision was made.

Explainable AI aims to close this gap by providing insight into how a machine learning model reaches its conclusions. It focuses on the development of algorithms and techniques that can provide human interpretable explanations, allowing users to understand the factors influencing model decisions. This transparency is critical in high-stakes industries such as healthcare, finance and law, where understanding the reasoning behind an AI system's decisions is essential for trust, accountability and regulatory compliance. Explainable AI uses different approaches depending on the specific model and problem domain. These include rule-based methods such as decision trees and rule extraction techniques that create explicit if-then statements to explain the model's decision-making process. Another approach is to use characteristic importance techniques, such as permutation importance or SHAP (Shapley Additive Explanations), which identify the relative contribution of input features to the output of the model.

In addition, surrogate models can be used to approximate the behavior of complex models, providing a more interpretable representation.

Deep Reinforcement Learning

Deep Reinforcement Learning (DRL) is an exciting and rapidly developing field of machine learning that combines elements of deep learning and reinforcement learning to enable intelligent agents to learn and make decisions in complex environments. Reinforcement learning typically focuses on training the agent to interact with the environment, learn from the feedback it receives, and optimize its actions to maximize the reward signal.

DRL takes this concept further by incorporating deep neural networks as feature approximators to handle high-dimensional input spaces. Using a deep learning architecture, DRL algorithms can efficiently process and extract features from raw sensory input such as images or sounds, allowing agents to learn directly from raw data without relying on manually created features. This allows DRL agents to work in various fields such as robotics, gaming, finance and autonomous vehicles. The basic principle of DRL is the use of an agent-environment interaction loop. The agent acts in the environment, receives feedback in the form of rewards or punishments, and uses this information to update its policy or value function to maximize the cumulative reward over time. The agent learns through trial and error by exploring the environment and finding optimal strategies or practices that lead to higher rewards.

One of the most important DRL techniques is the application of deep neural networks, commonly known as deep Q networks (DQNs). DQNs use deep convolutional neural networks to process visual inputs and evaluate the value of different actions in a given space. These networks are trained by an iterative process of experience repetition, where previous experiences are stored in the repetition memory and randomly selected during training to break temporal correlations in consecutive data.

Another important advance in DRL is the development of policy gradient methods such as proximal policy optimization (PPO) and trust region policy optimization (TRPO). These algorithms directly optimize the action of the agent by evaluating gradients and updating parameters to improve performance. Practical gradient methods have shown significant success in handling large-scale continuous operating states, making them suitable for tasks such as robot control and autonomous driving.

Despite its potential, DRL also faces challenges. Training DRL agents often requires significant computational resources and time because the sample is very complex and there are trade-offs between retrieval and use. In addition, issues such as sampling inefficiency, resistance to environmental changes, and security issues must be carefully addressed during actual deployment.

Generative Adversarial Networks (GANs)

Generative adversarial networks (GANs) are a type of machine learning model that has gained considerable attention and popularity in recent years. GANs are designed to produce new realistic data similar to a given training dataset. They consist of two main components: a generator network and a distribution network.

The generator network takes random noise as input and tries to produce synthetic data that resembles real training data. Its purpose is to create samples that are indistinguishable from real data, often images, audio or text. The generator learns to produce increasingly realistic samples by iteratively adapting its parameters based on feedback from the discriminator.

A discriminant network, on the other hand, acts as a classifier that tries to distinguish between real and generated data. It is taught on a dataset that includes real examples and generated examples. The discriminator learns to correctly classify the real data and generator output, while the generator tries to generate samples that deceive the discriminator into classifying them as real.

During the training process, the generator and discriminator networks compete with each other in a game-like scenario. The goal of the generator is to improve its ability to produce realistic samples, while the goal of the discriminator is to accurately distinguish between real and generated data. This competitive dynamic drives the learning process and helps both networks improve their performance over time.

Transfer Learning

Transfer learning is a powerful machine learning technique that uses knowledge from one domain or task to improve performance in another domain or task. It takes a pre-trained model, typically trained on a large dataset, and adapts it to limited labeled data for a new problem. By using information learned from the original task, transfer learning allows the model to better generalize and increase accuracy and efficiency.

The concept of transfer learning is based on the idea that many features learned in one task can be useful for solving another task. Instead of starting the learning process from scratch, transfer learning allows you to build a model based on information gathered from previous tasks. A pre-trained model, often a deep neural network, acts as a feature extractor that captures complex patterns and representations in the data. These learned features are then used as inputs to a new model, usually a shallow network or classifier, to solve the target problem.

There are different ways to implement transfer learning. One common approach is to use the pretrained model as a fixed feature extractor, where the weights of the pretrained layers are frozen and only the weights of the new layers are trained with the new task-specific information. This strategy is particularly effective when the new dataset is small and similar to the original dataset. By storing learned representations, the model can quickly adapt to a new task and achieve good results with less training data.

Federated Learning

Federated Learning is a revolutionary approach to machine learning that solves the challenges of distributed data learning models without the need to centralize data. Traditional machine learning methods require all data to be collected and transferred to a central server or cloud, which can be cumbersome, inefficient and cause data protection issues.

In contrast, Federated Learning allows models to be trained on multiple distributed devices, such as smartphones, Internet of Things (IoT) devices, or edge servers, while keeping the data local and secure. This approach exploits the computing power of the devices and uses their location data for training.

The federated learning process usually includes the following steps: First, the global model is initialized on the central server. Instead of sending the data to the server, the model is sent to the devices participating in the connected learning. Each device trains the model using its own location data, taking into account privacy constraints and preserving sensitive data. Locally trained models are then aggregated to a central server, typically using methods such as averaging or weighting to update the global model. This global model is then sent back to the devices and the process repeats, with the devices continuously improving the model in a collaborative manner.

Blended learning offers several advantages. This allows organizations to use massive amounts of distributed data without compromising privacy or security. Users retain control of their data as it resides on their devices, reducing the risk of data breaches. In addition, Federated Learning enables customized models that can be adapted to the user's individual preferences and local data characteristics, improving the user experience.

Edge Computing for Machine Learning

Machine learning edge computing refers to the practice of performing machine learning tasks and computing at the edge of the network, closer to the source of the data output, rather than relying solely on centralized cloud servers. It takes advantage of the ability of local devices such as smartphones, IoT devices or edge servers to process data and make real-time decisions locally without constant interaction with the cloud.

This approach offers several advantages for machine learning applications. First, by processing data at the edge, latency is significantly reduced because there is no need to send data back and forth to a remote server. This is particularly important for time-sensitive applications that require an immediate response, such as autonomous vehicles, industrial automation or real-time monitoring systems. Second, edge computing allows for better privacy and security. By keeping data processing and analysis closer to the source, sensitive data can be processed locally without moving to the cloud, reducing the risk of data breaches and ensuring compliance with data protection regulations. This is especially important in scenarios where privacy is a concern, such as healthcare or finance.

In addition, edge computing enables efficient use of network resources. During data preprocessing and initial analysis, only relevant data or summary results need to be sent to the cloud, reducing bandwidth requirements and overall network congestion. This can lead to cost savings and better scalability, especially in situations where network connections are limited or data volumes are large.

But edge computing in machine learning also presents some challenges. On-premises devices typically have limited computing power, memory capacity, and energy resources compared to cloud servers. Therefore, models must be optimized for these resource-constrained environments. Techniques such as model compression, quantization or truncation are often used to reduce model size and complexity without sacrificing accuracy. Moreover, managing and deploying machine learning models at the edge can be challenging, especially in heterogeneous environments with different devices and operating systems. Frameworks and tools are developed to simplify the deployment and organization of models across different edge devices, ensuring seamless integration and efficient use of resources.

Quantum Machine Learning

Quantum machine learning is an emerging field that combines the principles of quantum mechanics with machine learning algorithms to explore new computational techniques and solve complex problems more efficiently. It aims to exploit the unique properties of quantum systems, such as superposition and entanglement, to improve the capabilities of traditional machine learning methods.

In classical machine learning, data is processed and analyzed with classical computing systems that represent information as binary bits (0s and 1s) and operate them using classical logic gates. Quantum machine learning, on the other hand, uses quantum bits, or qubits, which can appear in a superposition of states and become entangled with other qubits. This allows quantum computers to perform calculations on exponentially larger amounts of data simultaneously, which can lead to significant acceleration of certain tasks. Quantum machine learning algorithms use quantum algorithms such as quantum Fourier transform and quantum phase estimation to process and process quantum data. These algorithms can be used for tasks such as clustering, classification, regression, and dimensionality reduction. For example, quantum support vector machines (SVMs) have been proposed as a quantum analogue of classical SVMs, aiming to provide faster and more accurate solutions to classification problems.

However, quantum machine learning is still in its infancy and there are several challenges to be overcome. One of the biggest challenges is noise and inconsistency in quantum systems, which can degrade computer performance. Researchers are investigating error correction techniques and developing quantum error correction codes to mitigate these effects. Another challenge is the limited number of qubits and the difficulty in scaling quantum systems to solve larger data sets and more complex problems.

Despite these challenges, quantum machine learning holds great promise for computationally demanding tasks such as optimization, chemistry, finance, and cryptography. It could revolutionize the approach to machine learning, offering exponential speed and new algorithms that can solve problems beyond the capabilities of classical computers. Continued research and development of quantum technologies should further unleash the power of quantum machine learning in the future.

8.2. DEEP LEARNING AND NEURAL ARCHITECTURE ADVANCEMENTS

Recent developments in deep learning and neural architecture have significantly contributed to the growth of machine learning. These developments have produced ground-breaking work in a number of fields, including speech recognition, natural language processing, and computer vision.

Convolutional Neural Networks (CNNs)

Convolutional neural networks (CNN) have revolutionized the field of machine learning, especially computer vision. CNNs are a type of deep learning model designed to process and analyze visual data such as images and videos by mimicking biological processes in the human visual cortex.

At the heart of CNNs are convolutional layers that apply learning filters to the input data. These filters detect patterns and features in the input image at different spatial scales. By converging these filters over an image, the network can capture local relationships and hierarchical representations, enabling the detection of complex patterns and objects. CNNs also contain pooling layers that reduce the feature maps produced by the convolutional layers. Combining helps to reduce the spatial dimensions of the data while preserving important features, making the network more robust to variations in location and extent. Common pooling techniques include max pooling, average pooling and sum pooling.

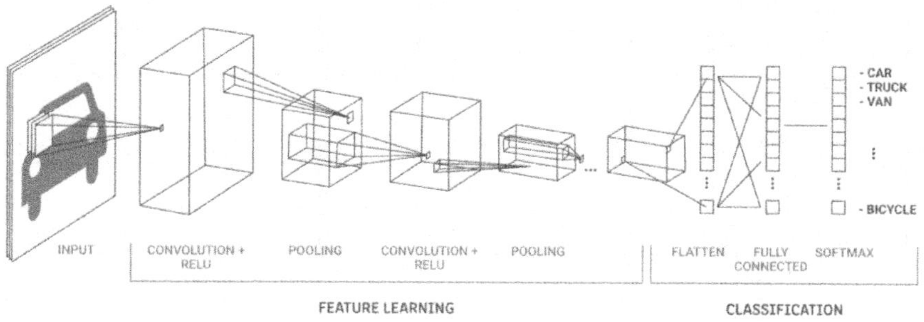

Convolutional Neural Networks (CNNs)

In addition, CNNs often include fully connected layers at the end of the network that perform classification or regression tasks based on learned features. These fully connected layers take the output of the convolution and pooling layers and feed it into a traditional neural network architecture, allowing the network to make predictions based on the extracted features. The success of CNNs stems from their ability to automatically learn and extract meaningful features from raw visual data. By training on large datasets, CNNs can learn to recognize complex visual patterns and generalize to unseen data. This makes CNNs particularly suitable for many computer vision tasks, including image classification, object detection, semantic segmentation, and image generation.

CNNs have also been used outside of computer vision, finding utility in areas such as natural language processing and time series analysis. For example, in NLP, CNNs can be used to process and analyze text data by treating it as a one-dimensional sequence of words or characters. In conclusion, CNNs have had a great impact in the field of machine learning, especially in the field of computer vision. They excel at automatically learning and extracting features from visual data, enabling tasks such as image classification and object detection. Their ability to capture hierarchical representations and their flexibility for application in other domains have made CNNs a powerful tool in the machine learning toolbox.

Table 1: CNN Architecture Layers

Layer Type	Output Shape	Parameters
Input	(32, 32, 3)	-
Convolutional	(28, 28, 32)	896
Activation	(28, 28, 32)	-
Max Pooling	(14, 14, 32)	-
Convolutional	(10, 10, 64)	51,264
Activation	(10, 10, 64)	-
Max Pooling	(5, 5, 64)	-
Flatten	1600	-
Dense	256	410,496
Activation	256	-
Dense	10	2,570
Activation	10	-

Recurrent Neural Networks (RNNs)

Recurrent Neural Networks (RNN) are a class of neural networks widely used in machine learning for tasks involving sequential data. Unlike feedforward neural networks, which process input data independently, RNNs are designed to process sequential information, maintaining an internal memory or "latent state" that allows them to pick up dependencies and patterns over time.

A key feature of RNNs is their ability to work with sequences of variable length. This makes them suitable for tasks such as natural language processing, speech recognition, machine translation, sentiment analysis and time series forecasting. In these fields, the order of the input data is critical, and RNNs excel at capturing temporal dynamics and context within sequences. The basic building block of an RNN is a recurrent cell that processes one element of the input sequence at a time while maintaining its internal state. The most commonly used recurrent cell is LSTM (Long Short-Term Memory), which contains input mechanisms that control information flow and gradients throughout the network. Another popular variant is the Gated Recurrent Unit (GRU), which simplifies the LSTM architecture by combining forget and feed gates.

During training, RNNs are optimized using methods such as backpropagation through time (BPTT), which extends backpropagation to process sequences. BPTT calculates the gradients of the loss function with respect to the network parameters by unwrapping and moving back the gradients during the time of the iterative calculation. One of the challenges of RNNs is the vanishing or exploding gradient problem, which can occur when the gradients become too small or too large during training, causing difficulty in learning long-term dependencies. Methods such as gradient clipping, weight restoration strategies, and the use of alternative recurrent cells such as LSTM and GRU have been proposed to alleviate this problem.

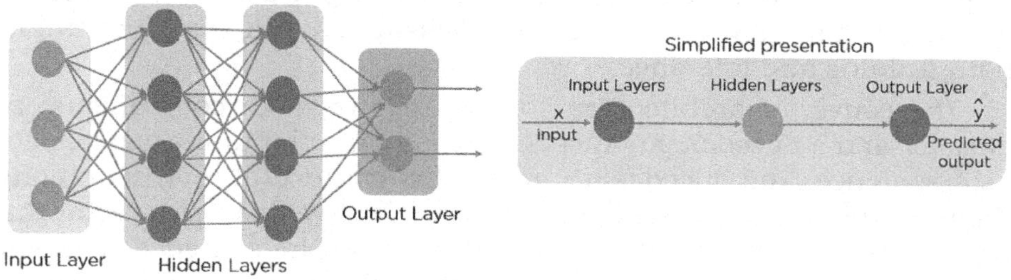

Recurrent Neural Networks (RNN)

In recent years, variants of RNNs have been developed to address certain limitations. For example, the attention mechanism improves the ability of RNNs to focus on relevant parts of the input sequence, and transformer-based architectures have gained popularity in natural language processing tasks by replacing recurrent connections with self-monitoring mechanisms.

Overall, RNNs have proven to be powerful models of sequential data processing, enabling machines to understand and generate human language, predict future events, and make informed decisions based on temporal patterns. Their flexibility, adaptability and ability to capture dependencies over time make them a valuable tool in various areas of machine learning and artificial intelligence.

Table 2: LSTM Cell Components

Component	Description
Input Gate	Controls the flow of information into memory
Forget Gate	Controls the forgetting of previous memory
Cell State	Holds and updates the memory
Output Gate	Controls the output of the cell

Transformer Architecture

The Transformer architecture is a prominent model in the field of machine learning, especially in the field of natural language processing (NLP). It has revolutionized various NLP tasks and significantly improved advanced results. Introduced by Vaswani et al. In 2017, the Transformer model proposed a new approach to sequence-to-sequence learning without relying on recurrent neural networks (RNNs).

At the core of Transformer's architecture is a self-aware mechanism that allows the model to capture dependencies between different words in a sentence. Unlike traditional repetition models that process sequential data one by one, Transformer can process all the words in a sentence simultaneously. This parallelism makes it very powerful for both training and inference.

The converter architecture consists of two main components: an encoder and a decoder. An encoder processes an input sequence, such as a sentence, and encodes it into a set of contextual representations. Each word in the input sequence is converted to a fixed-size vector that represents its meaning in the context of the entire sentence. The self-attention mechanism plays a crucial role in this process, as it assigns a different weight to each word depending on how it relates to other words in the sentence.

The decoder component takes the encoded representations generated by the encoder and forms an output sequence. It uses a similar introspective mechanism to run the input sequence and predict the next word in the output sequence. During training, the model is taught to generate the correct target sequence by maximizing the likelihood of the target sequence with the input sequence.

One of the main advantages of the Transformer architecture is its ability to capture the long-range dependencies of a statement more efficiently than traditional recursive models. This is achieved by a self-aware mechanism that allows the model to assign more weight to meaningful words regardless of their position in the sequence. As a result, Transformer has shown excellent performance in tasks such as machine translation, text summarization and language generation.

Table 3: Transformer Architecture Components

Component	Description
Encoder	Processes input sequences using self-attention layers
Decoder	Generates output sequences using masked self-attention
Multi-head Attention	Allows the model to focus on different positions
Feed-Forward Networks	Applies non-linear transformations to each position

8.3. INTERPRETABLE MODELS AND EXPLAINABLE AI

Important machine learning ideas like Interpretable Models and Explainable AI (XAI) seek to make sophisticated models' decision-making processes transparent and understandable

Interpretable Models

Interpretable models in machine learning refer to algorithms and techniques that provide understandable and transparent explanations for their predictions or decisions. As machine learning models become increasingly sophisticated and powerful, there is a need to understand what drives their results, especially in critical applications such as healthcare, finance and law.

Interpretability is important for several reasons. First, it promotes trust and acceptance of machine learning systems by providing users and stakeholders with information about how the models arrive at their conclusions. This transparency allows users to identify potential biases, errors or limitations, leading to more informed decisions. Second, interpretability helps meet legal and ethical requirements, as many statutes require explanations for automated decisions affecting individuals.

There are several techniques for achieving interpretability in machine learning models. Linear models such as linear regression and logistic regression are inherently interpretable because their coefficients represent the significance and direction of each characteristic. Decision trees and rule-based models also provide interpretation because they can be represented as a set of if-else statements, making decision-making easy to understand.

Another approach is to use simplified or "surrogate" models that approximate the behavior of complex models. These substitute models are often simpler and more interpretable, and provide insight into the decision-making process of the original model. They can be trained on the same dataset or a smaller dataset. Recent advances in interpretability research have focused on the development of techniques for deep learning models, which are notorious for their complexity and lack of interpretability. Methods such as LIME (Local Interpretable Model Agnostic Explanations) and SHAP (SHapley additive Explanations) were introduced to explain the predictions of black-box models by evaluating their behavior in local regions of the input space.

Explainable AI (XAI)

Explainable AI (XAI) refers to the concept and techniques in the field of machine learning that aim to provide understandable and transparent explanations for the decisions and predictions made by artificial intelligence models. Although machine learning models have shown excellent performance in various tasks, their inherent complexity often makes it difficult to understand the reasons behind their decisions, especially in complex deep learning models such as neural networks. This lack of interpretability can be particularly problematic in critical sectors such as health, finance and law, where transparency and accountability are crucial.

XAI methods aim to bridge this gap by enabling people to understand and trust the decisions of AI systems. These methods include a variety of techniques, including rule-based models, feature importance analysis, model-agnostic methods, and model-specific approaches. Rule-based models provide clear, interpretable rules that guide the decision-making process, allowing people to follow the decision logic step by step. Characteristic importance analysis techniques identify and quantify the relative contributions of different input features to modeling predictions and shed light on the factors influencing the results.

Model diagnostic methods, on the other hand, aim to explain the behavior of any black-box model without relying on the internal details of the model. Techniques such as LIME (Local Interpretable Model-Agnostic

Explanations) and SHAP (SHapley Additive Explanations) generate local explanations by evaluating the behavior of the model in a specific region of the input space. These explanations highlight important features of individual forecasts and provide insight into the decision-making process. Model-specific approaches focus on improving interpretability in certain types of models, such as decision trees or neural networks. Interpretability is inherent in decision making because decisions are based on if-else rules. In neural networks, techniques such as attention mechanisms, layered importance propagation (LRP), and saliency maps help identify the most important input features and emphasize their impact on the final decision.

Overall, the goal of the XAI industry is to find a balance between the accuracy and complexity of AI models and human interpretability. By providing understandable explanations for AI decisions, XAI methods can increase transparency, build trust, and empower people to understand and validate the outputs of AI systems. This is particularly important in critical areas where lives, rights or important resources are at risk. Ultimately, XAI contributes to the broader goal of responsible and ethical AI adoption by empowering users and stakeholders to make informed decisions based on a clear understanding of the behavior of AI models.

8.4. FEDERATED LEARNING AND PRIVACY-PRESERVING MACHINE LEARNING

Federated Learning

Federated learning is a distributed approach to machine learning that allows multiple parties to work together to train a model without sharing raw data. In traditional machine learning, data is usually collected from various sources, centralized, and then used to train a model. However, in the case of connected learning, the training process takes place on local devices or servers, where the information is stored, which preserves privacy and security.

The federated learning starts by sharing the base model to each participating device or server. These devices train the model independently using local data without transmitting the raw data to a central server. Instead, only updated model parameters or gradients are shared with the central server or coordinator. The server aggregates updates from all participants and computes a new global model by combining the local updates. This global model is then sent back to the participants, who continue to train and refresh locally.

Blended learning offers several advantages over traditional centralized approaches. One of the most important advantages is the preservation of privacy, because the original data remains on the devices where it was produced. This is especially important when dealing with sensitive or personal information. Since there is no need to transfer data to a central server, the risk of data breaches or unauthorized use is greatly reduced.

Another advantage of blended learning is better scalability. Large-scale machine learning models can be trained on many distributed devices or servers, enabling efficient processing of massive data sets without extensive data transfers.

Blended learning also promotes collaboration and participation. This allows multiple parties, such as individuals, organizations or devices, to participate in the model training process. This decentralized nature encourages broad participation, resulting in diverse and representative designs.

Overall, blended learning is a promising approach to enable collaborative machine learning while maintaining data privacy and security. This could revolutionize the industry, allowing organizations and individuals to benefit from shared data while maintaining control over their own data.

Component	Description
Centralized Model Training	Traditional approach where data is collected centrally
Federated Learning	Training happens locally on decentralized devices
Communication	Model updates are sent from devices to a central server
Privacy Preservation	Data stays on user devices, reducing privacy concerns
Scalability	Suitable for large-scale applications and edge devices
Collaborative Learning	Enables multiple parties to contribute to model training

Privacy-Preserving Machine Learning

Privacy-preserving machine learning refers to a set of techniques and approaches that aim to ensure the privacy of sensitive data by enabling the training and decision-making of machine learning models. Due to the growing demand for data-driven applications and growing data protection concerns, attention has been paid to privacy preserving machine learning.

One of the main challenges in machine learning is the need for large amounts of data to train accurate models. However, this often requires the sharing of sensitive information such as personal, medical or financial information, which may compromise an individual's privacy. Privacy-preserving machine learning aims to solve this problem by developing methods that allow organizations and individuals to collaborate and extract meaningful insights from data without revealing the underlying sensitive information. There are a number of techniques used in privacy-preserving machine learning. One common approach is differential privacy, which adds controlled noise to the data to provide statistical guarantees of privacy. This ensures that the presence or absence of certain data points does not significantly affect the production of the model, thus protecting the privacy of an individual.

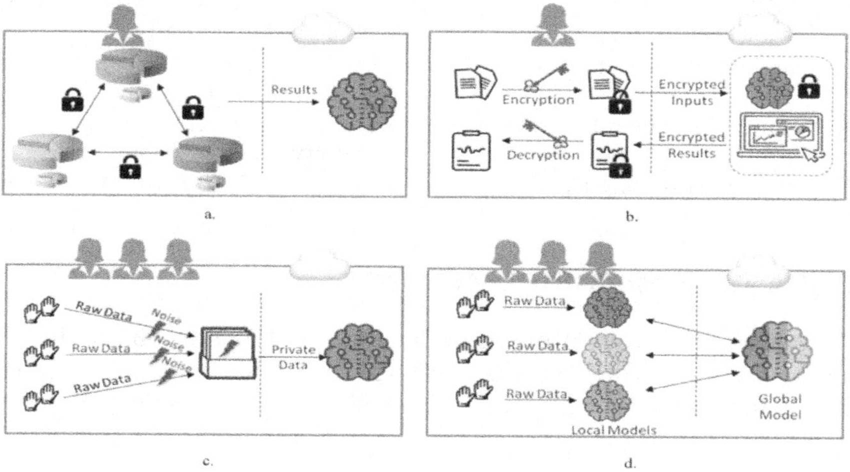

Privacy-Preserving Machine Learning

Another approach is secure multiparty computation (MPC), which allows multiple parties to jointly compute a function on their private inputs without revealing the inputs to each other. This technique enables a collaborative training model without disclosing the original data to any party. Homomorphic encryption is another privacy-preserving machine learning method. It enables computation of encrypted data, which allows machine learning models to be trained and inferred without encrypting sensitive data. This ensures confidentiality of information throughout the process.

Associative learning is another popular method in privacy-preserving machine learning. It includes training models for multiple distributed devices or servers without data transmission. Instead, only model updates or gradients are exchanged, preserving individual data privacy.

These technologies offer different levels of privacy guarantees and their choice depends on the specific requirements and constraints of the application. Privacy-preserving machine learning plays a key role in industries where data protection is critical, such as healthcare, finance and telecommunications. By enabling organizations to collaborate and gain insights without compromising privacy, these technologies promote the responsible and ethical use of data in machine learning applications.

Technique	Description
Differential Privacy	Adds noise to data to protect individual privacy
Secure Multi-Party Computation	Allows parties to compute jointly without revealing inputs
Homomorphic Encryption	Enables computations on encrypted data without decryption
Federated Encrypted Learning	Combines federated learning and encryption techniques
Privacy-Preserving Deep Learning	Techniques specific to neural networks

8.5. QUANTUM MACHINE LEARNING

The area of quantum machine learning (QML) combines ideas from machine learning with quantum physics. It tries to improve machine learning methods by utilising the special characteristics of quantum systems.

Introduction to Quantum Machine Learning

Quantum Machine Learning (QML) is an emerging field at the intersection of quantum computing and machine learning. It combines the principles of quantum mechanics with the power of classical machine learning algorithms and aims to exploit the unique properties of quantum systems to improve the capabilities of traditional machine learning methods. QML aims to explore and exploit the potential of quantum computers to solve complex computational problems more efficiently than classical computers.

In traditional machine learning, algorithms process and analyze data using classical bits, which can be either zero or 1. Quantum computing, on the other hand, uses quantum bits or qubits, which in principle can simultaneously represent both 0 and 1 of superposition. This property allows quantum computers to perform parallel computations and potentially provide exponential speedup for certain tasks.

In the context of QML, quantum algorithms are designed to process quantum data, make predictions, and perform optimization tasks using quantum resources. This includes quantum circuits, quantum gates and designs with quantum effects. Quantum algorithms such as quantum support vector machine, quantum neural networks and quantum variational algorithms have been proposed to solve classification, regression, clustering and generative modeling problems.

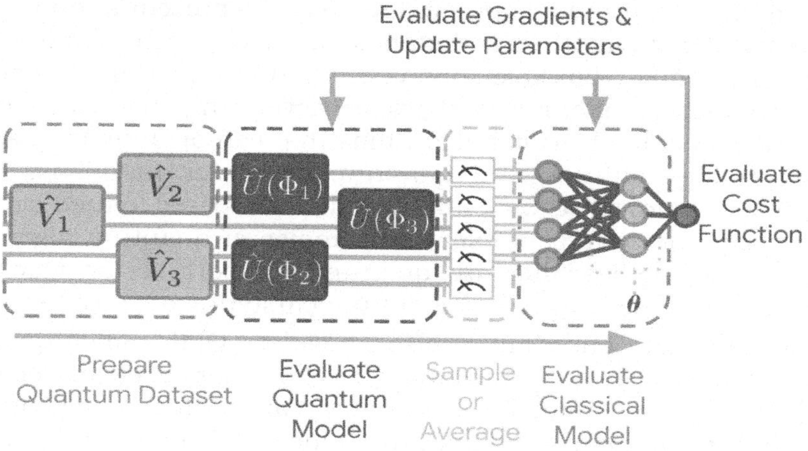

Quantum Machine Learning

QML faces many challenges, including the need for error correction to reduce the effects of noise and inconsistency in quantum systems. Furthermore, using and manipulating large quantum processors is still technically demanding. However, researchers and industry experts are actively exploring the potential of QML for certain problems that can benefit from the advantages of quantum computing, such as optimization, cryptography, and drug discovery.

As the field advances, QML can revolutionize machine learning by solving complex problems that are difficult to solve on classical computers. Using quantum properties such as entanglement and superposition, QML enables more accurate predictions, faster computations and new machine learning methods. As quantum hardware advances and more robust algorithms are developed, the future of QML promises to open new frontiers in machine learning and artificial intelligence.

Key Components of Quantum Machine Learning

Quantum Machine Learning (QML) combines the principles of quantum mechanics with the field of machine learning, which opens up new ways to solve complex computational problems. It aims to exploit the unique properties of quantum systems to improve the efficiency and capabilities of traditional machine learning algorithms.

One of the core components of quantum machine learning is quantum computing. Quantum computers use superposition and entanglement to manipulate and process data in ways that are fundamentally different from classical computers. By using quantum bits, or qubits, instead of classical bits, quantum computers are able to represent and process a huge amount of information simultaneously, allowing the simultaneous exploration of many possible solutions. Another important component is quantum algorithms. Researchers are developing quantum versions of classical machine learning algorithms that can operate on quantum data and take advantage of quantum computer functions. These algorithms can provide exponential speedup compared to their classical counterparts for certain problems. Examples of quantum algorithms used in machine learning are quantum support vector machines, quantum neural networks, and quantum clustering algorithms.

Quantum data encoding is also crucial in QML. Since quantum computers operate in quantum states, it is necessary to encode classical data into quantum states for processing. Various techniques such as quantum function maps and quantum pins are being explored to map classical information into quantum states. These coding methods play an important role in harnessing the power of quantum computers for machine learning tasks.

In addition, quantum machine learning requires specialized hardware and infrastructure. Quantum computers are still in development and not yet widely available. However, efforts are underway to build quantum processors with increasing qubit numbers and improved coherence times. Additionally, quantum simulators and quantum programming languages are needed to facilitate the development and testing of quantum machine learning algorithms.

Finally, quantum machin e learning involves the integration of classical and quantum c o mponents. Hybrid approaches combining classical machine learn i ng and quantum computing are being explored to overcome th e limitations of current quantum hardware. These hybrid designs aim to exploit the strengths of both classical and quantum systems, with classical computers handling pre-processing, post-processing and cer t ain computational tasks, while quantum computers focus on basic quantum computations. In short, the core components of quantum machine learning are quantum computing, quantum algorithms, quantum data encoding, specialized devices and infrastructure, and the integration of classical and quantum components. Together, these components open the way to exploiting the unique properties of quantum systems to revolutionize the field of machine learning and solve complex problems that are currently beyond the reach of classical approaches.

Potential Benefits of Quantum Machine Learning

Quantum Machine Learning (QML) can transform traditional machine learning methods by exploiting the unique properties of quantum mechanics. By combining the principles of quantum physics with the power of machine learning algorithms, QML offers several potential advantages.

One of the main advantages of QML is its ability to process and analyze large amounts of data much faster than conventional computers. Quantum computers exploit quantum parallelism and superposition to perform calculations in multiple states simultaneously, allowing them to explore a much larger solution space and speed up computational tasks. This acceleration can significantly improve the training efficiency of complex machine learning models and enable real-time analysis of large data sets. In addition, QML can solve computational problems related to high-dimensional feature spaces. Classic machine learning algorithms struggle with computational demands that grow exponentially as the number of features increases. On the other hand, quantum algorithms can use quantum mixing and quantum spatial compression to efficiently represent and process high-dimensional data, enabling more accurate and faster learning.

Another advantage of QML is its potential to improve model generalization. Quantum computers can take advantage of quantum disorder and quantum coherence to better deal with noise and uncertainty in data. This feature opens the door to older, more accurate models that can effectively handle noisy, incomplete or ambiguous data sets, enabling better predictions and decision making.

In addition, QML has the ability to solve optimization problems more efficiently. Many machine learning tasks involve optimizing objective functions or finding optimal parameters. Quantum algorithms such as quantum annealing or variational quantum algorithms can use quantum tunnels and quantum fluctuations to explore and converge to optimal solutions more efficiently than classical optimization methods. This can lead to faster convergence, better model performance and shorter training. Overall, the potential benefits of quantum machine learning are enormous. From accelerated data processing and analysis to advanced model generalization and more efficient optimization, QML promises to open new frontiers in machine learning and advance fields including healthcare, finance, materials science and optimization-based industries. However, it is important to note that QML is still a developing field, and practical applications and their full potential are yet to be fully realized.

Despite having immense potential, quantum machine learning is still in its infancy. To realise the full potential of this fascinating topic, researchers and practitioners are constantly exploring and improving quantum algorithms and structures.

8.6. EDGE COMPUTING AND IOT INTEGRATION WITH MACHINE LEARNING

A paradigm known as "edge computing" moves computation and data storage closer to the point of data production. Instead of transferring data to a centralised cloud server, it processes it at or close to the edge devices to minimise latency, increase security, and increase efficiency. The term "Internet of Things" (IoT) describes a network of physically connected objects that communicate and collect data. Edge computing and the Internet of Things can offer real-time analysis, intelligent decision-making, and predictive capabilities at the network's edge when paired with machine learning.

Edge Computing

Edge computing in machine learning refers to the practice of performing data processing and analysis at the edge of the network, closer to the source of data generation, rather than relying solely on centralized cloud servers or data centers. It aims to overcome the limitations of traditional cloud-based architectures, where data is sent to a remote server for processing and then returned with the results.

Using edge computing, machine learning models can be implemented and used directly on local devices such as sensors, smartphones or edge servers. This proximity to the data source offers several important advantages. First, it reduces the latency associated with sending data to a remote server, enabling real-time or near-real-time decision making. This is particularly important for time-sensitive applications such as autonomous vehicles, industrial automation and remote monitoring.

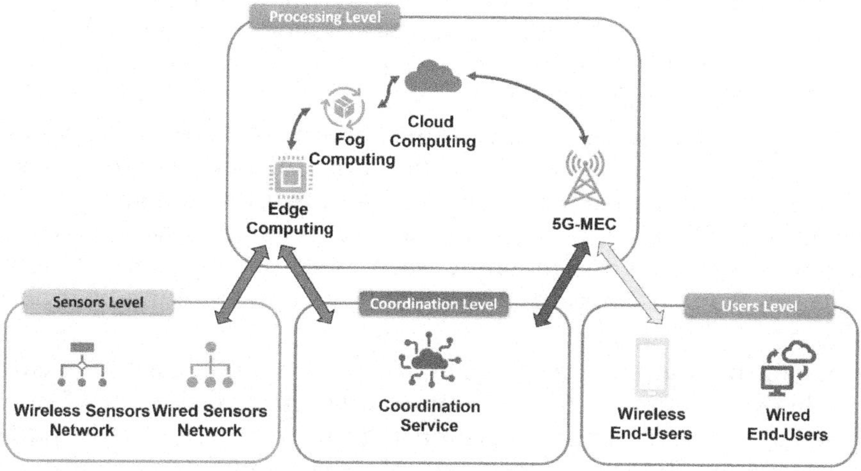

Edge Computing for IoT Integration

In addition, edge computing in machine learning meets the challenge of processing large volumes of data. Instead of sending huge amounts of raw data to the cloud, only relevant or pre-processed information is sent. This minimizes bandwidth requirements and reduces associated costs. In addition, it improves data privacy and security by keeping sensitive data in a local environment, reducing exposure to potential vulnerabilities during data transmission. Edge computing also improves machine learning capabilities by enabling local model training and inference. Models can be trained using data collected locally on edge devices, which is particularly useful when there is limited or intermittent cloud connectivity. This localized training enables individualized and adaptive models that can be adapted to the user's individual preferences or changing environmental conditions.

Overall, machine learning edge computing brings the power of AI closer to the edge of the network, enabling real-time decision-making, lower latency, lower bandwidth requirements, better privacy and security, and distributed learning capabilities. It has the potential to revolutionize multiple industries by enabling intelligent and autonomous systems that can operate efficiently and effectively in edge environments.

IoT (Internet of Things)

Integrating IoT (Internet of Things) with machine learning means combining two powerful technologies to enable intelligent data analysis and decision making across connected devices. IoT involves connecting various physical devices, sensors and actuators, allowing them to collect and exchange information over the Internet. Machine learning, on the other hand, uses algorithms and statistical models to gain insights and patterns from data, allowing systems to make predictions and operate without specialized programming.

When IoT and machine learning are combined, it creates a synergistic relationship that enhances the capabilities of both technologies. IoT generates massive amounts of real-time data from sensors embedded in devices, such as temperature, humidity, pressure and location data. This data is then fed into machine learning algorithms that can analyze and learn from it to gain meaningful insights and make informed decisions.

One of the main applications of IoT integration in machine learning is predictive maintenance. By continuously monitoring data from IoT-enabled devices, machine learning algorithms can identify patterns and anomalies that indicate potential device failures or maintenance needs. This enables preventive maintenance, minimizes downtime and reduces costs.

Another application is in smart homes and cities, where IoT devices collect information about energy consumption, traffic patterns, air quality and more. Machine learning algorithms can process this data to optimize energy use, improve traffic management and overall city planning.

In the healthcare industry, integrating the Internet of Things with machine learning enables remote patient monitoring, early disease detection and individualized treatment. Wearable devices and sensors collect real-time health data, which machine learning algorithms analyze to identify abnormal patterns or predict health risks, enabling timely interventions and better outcomes for patients.

Table 4: Comparison of Edge Computing, and IoT Integration with Machine Learning

	Edge Computing	**IoT Integration with ML**
Latency	Lower	Lower
Bandwidth Usage	Optimized	Optimized
Security and Privacy	Improved	Improved
Offline Capabilities	Supported	Supported
Real-time Decision-making	Real-time	Real-time
Scalability	Limited	High
Cost	Lower	Variable

There are many advantages to the combination of edge computing, IoT, and machine learning, including decreased latency, optimised bandwidth utilisation, enhanced security, and localised decision-making. Real-time analysis and intelligent decision-making are made feasible by processing data at the edge devices, opening up a wide range of applications across numerous industries.

8.7. MACHINE LEARNING ETHICS AND FAIRNESS

Fairness and machine learning ethics are crucial factors to take into account while developing and deploying machine learning systems. They require ensuring that the machine learning models and algorithms are fair, transparent, and considerate of privacy, as well as that the decisions and results that follow are just and equitable

Bias and Discrimination

Machine learning bias and discrimination refers to the existence and persistence of unfairness and bias in automated systems. Machine learning algorithms are designed to learn from large data sets and make predictions or decisions about the data based on the patterns and correlations they find. However, these algorithms are not immune to biases and biases in the training data or the way they are programmed.

One of the biases of machine learning is data bias. If the training data used to develop the algorithm is not representative or contains inherent biases, the algorithm may inadvertently learn and retain those biases. For example, if a facial recognition system is trained primarily on data from light-skinned people, it may struggle to accurately recognize or classify the faces of people with darker skin tones. This can lead to discriminatory consequences, such as misidentifying individuals or excluding them from certain services or opportunities based on their race or ethnicity.

Algorithmic bias can also arise from the characteristics and variables used in the training process. If certain characteristics are highly correlated with protected characteristics, such as race, gender, or age, the algorithm may inadvertently rely on those characteristics when making predictions, leading to discriminatory results. For example, if a hiring decision algorithm learns that certain words or phrases commonly used in resumes are correlated with gender, it may favor or exclude applicants based on gender, even if that was not the intention. In addition, the design and implementation of machine learning systems can be affected by developer biases or a lack of diversity in development teams. If the perspectives, experiences and values of marginalized groups are not sufficiently considered in the develo p ment process, the resulting algorithms can perpetuate existing social prejudices and discrimination.

Addressing bias and discrimination in machine learning requires a multifaceted approach. This includes careful maintenance of diverse and representative training data, regular review and evaluation of algorithms for biases, and the use of techniques such as fairness-aware learning and algorithm transparency. Additionally, promoting diversity and inclusion in development teams can help mitigate bias and ensure fairer and more unbiased algorithms are created. Overall, understanding and addressing bias and discrimination in machine learning is critical to ensuring that these technologies promote fairness, equity, and social justice, rather than reinforcing existing biases and inequalities in society.

Applicant	**Gender**	**Education Level**	**Loan Approved**
A	Female	High School	No
B	Male	College	Yes
C	Female	College	No
D	Male	High School	Yes

All of the female applicants in this table have had their loan requests declined, suggesting that there is a gender bias in loan approval. Fairness must be ensured in algorithm design, data collecting, and preprocessing when addressing bias.

Transparency and Explainability

Transparency and explainability of machine learning refers to the ability to understand and interpret how a machine learning model arrives at its predictions or decisions. As machine learning algorithms become increasingly complex and powerful, there is a growing need to ensure that their results are not only accurate, but also explainable and transparent.

Transparency refers to the ability to shed light on the inner workings of a machine learning model. This includes providing information about the data used to train the model, the properties or variables observed, and the decision-making process of the algorithm. Transparency allows users and stakeholders to understand the factors influencing the model's outputs, which ensures accountability and confidence in its predictions. Explainability, on the other hand, focuses on providing humanly understandable explanations for the model's predictions or decisions. It aims to bridge the gap between the "black box" nature of complex machine learning algorithms and human understanding. Explanatory models provide insight into the key features or patterns that drive the model's results, allowing users to validate the model's conclusions and diagnose potential anomalies or errors.

The importance of transparency and explainability in machine learning stems from several reasons. First, it is essential for enforcing legislation in sensitive areas such as health, finance and law, where decisions have a significant impact on the lives of individuals. In addition, transparency and explainability facilitate the acceptance and adoption of machine learning systems by eliminating their decision-making process and increasing trust.

Privacy and Data Protection

Privacy and data protection in machine learning are critical considerations that require careful attention and consideration. Machine learning algorithms rely on massive amounts of data to train and make accurate predictions or decisions. This information often includes personal and sensitive information such as personal identifiers, health information, financial information and browsing history. Therefore, ensuring the privacy and protection of this information is of utmost importance.

One of the most important challenges in machine learning is finding a balance between harnessing the power of data to gain valuable insights and protecting the privacy of individuals. Organizations must adhere to strong data protection frameworks and regulations, such as the European Union's General Data Protection Regulation (GDPR), to protect individuals' data. These frameworks define the principles of legal and fair data processing, including obtaining informed consent, limiting the purpose of use, minimizing data and implementing appropriate safeguards.

Anonymous and pseudonymization techniques play a crucial role in protecting privacy during the data processing phase. Anonymization means removing personally identifiable information (PII) from data sets so that individuals cannot be re-identified. Pseudonymization, on the other hand, replaces identifiable data with artificial identifiers, allowing the data to be analyzed while maintaining a level of privacy. In addition, it is important for machine learning systems to follow the principles of privacy by design. This approach involves integrating privacy and data protection measures into the system architecture and development process from the start. Organizations can minimize privacy risks and improve privacy by considering privacy implications at every stage, from data collection and storage to model training and deployment.

Another important aspect is the transparency and explainability of machine learning models. As these models become increasingly sophisticated, it is important to understand how they make decisions and identify potential biases or unfair outcomes. By promoting transparency, individuals can better understand how their data is used and assess the potential risks associated with its use.

To ensure compliance with privacy and data protection regulations, organizations must implement sound data management practices. This includes keeping clear data records, establishing data retention policies and conducting regular audits to ensure compliance with privacy rules and regulations. Furthermore, giving individuals access to their data and control over its use, including the ability to delete or modify it, is consistent with respect for their privacy rights.

Fairness Metrics and Evaluation

Fairness metrics and evaluation in machine learning refers to the assessment of algorithmic fairness and the measurement of potential biases in the implementation of machine learning models. As machine learning algorithms play an increasingly important role in decision-making processes in various fields, it is very important to ensure that their results are fair and impartial, respecting ethical and legal considerations.

Fairness metrics provide a quantitative approach to assess and quantify biases in machine learning models. These metrics generally measure differences in predictions and outcomes between different groups based on protected characteristics such as race, gender, age, or religion. Some commonly used measures of fairness are disparate effects, equal probability, and statistical equality difference. These metrics allow researchers and practitioners to assess the extent to which a model may exhibit discriminatory behavior.

Mitigating Bias and Ensuring Fairness

Mitigating errors and ensuring fairness in machine learning is a critical and ongoing challenge in the field of artificial intelligence. Bias refers to the presence of systematic errors or biases in data, algorithms or decision-making processes that can lead to unfair results or discrimination against certain groups of people. This bias can be inadvertently built into machine learning systems due to a number of factors, such as biased training data, faulty algorithms, or biased human judgments used to label the training data.

Several approaches are used to solve this problem. First, it is important that we have diverse and representative educational data that covers diverse demographics and perspectives. This helps reduce the risk of skewed or incomplete data that can reinforce existing biases. In addition, researchers are developing techniques to identify and quantify biases in machine learning models, enabling assessment of potential unfairness.

Another approach involves refining the algorithms themselves to minimize bias. This can be achieved through techniques such as regularization, which adds constraints to the learning process to prevent the reinforcement of distorted patterns. Reciprocal training is another strategy in which models are trained to distinguish sensitive characteristics (such as gender or race) from the desired output, thus reducing the model's dependence on such characteristics. Transparency and interpretability are critical when dealing with machine learning biases. The decision-making process of AI systems has become more understandable and interpretable, making it easier to identify and correct biased results. Researchers are developing methods to explain the reasoning behind AI predictions and provide insight into the factors that influence those predictions.

It's critical to remember that research in the fields of ethics and justice in machine learning is challenging and dynamic. Depending on the situation and application domain, specific concerns and techniques may change. To properly handle these issues, multidisciplinary cooperation with specialists from numerous domains, including ethics, law, and social sciences, is essential.

8.8 HUMAN-CENTRIC MACHINE LEARNING

A branch of machine learning called "human-centric machine learning" (HCML) aims to create algorithms and models that are easier for people to comprehend, transparent, and apply. The objective is to develop machine learning algorithms that can work well in tandem with people, enabling better judgement, enhanced customer happiness, and improved trust.

Interpretability and Explainability

Interpretability and explainability are important aspects of machine learning that aim to provide insight into how algorithms make predictions or decisions. As machine learning models become more sophisticated, the need to understand and trust their behavior grows, especially in high-stakes industries such as healthcare, finance and autonomous systems.

Interpretability refers to the ability to understand and interpret the reasoning behind the model's predictions. This involves uncovering the underlying patterns, relationships and factors that influence the output of the model. After understanding the model's decision making, interpretability helps users assess the reliability of the model, identify biases, and identify potential errors or weaknesses. Explainability, on the other hand, focuses on providing a human-understandable explanation for the output of the model. It goes beyond understanding the inner workings of a model and aims to present a clear and coherent rationale that users can easily understand without a deep understanding of machine learning. Explainable techniques aim to bridge the gap between the complex calculations performed by algorithms and the human-level understanding needed to make decisions.

Several methods have been developed to improve the interpretability and explainability of machine learning. These include feature importance analysis, which quantifies the contribution of each input feature to the model's output, and rule extraction, which extracts human-readable rules from black-box models. Visualizations such as heatmaps, decision trees, and visibility maps can also help interpret and explain the behavior of models.

Interpretability and explainability not only help users understand and trust machine learning models, but also enable regulatory compliance and ethical considerations. They enable the identification and mitigation of model bias and unfairness and ensure that projections are transparent and accountable. In addition, they make it easier for domain experts to collaborate with machine learning practitioners, allowing valuable information and feedback to be included in the model development process.

Method	**Description**
Feature Importance	Identifying the most important features that contribute to the predictions.
Rule-based Models	Using a set of if-then rules to explain the decision-making process.
Local Explanations	Providing explanations for individual predictions using techniques like LIME.
Model Distillation	Training simpler models to mimic the behavior of complex models.
Visualizations	Using visual representations like heatmaps or decision trees for explanation.

Human-in-the-Loop Machine Learning

Human-in-the-loop machine learning (HIL ML) is an approach that combines the power of machine learning algorithms with human expertise and supervision to improve the overall performance and accuracy of machine learning models. It involves the active participation of humans in the training, validation and decision-making processes of machine learning systems.

In traditional machine learning workflows, models are trained on large data sets, and once deployed, they operate autonomously and make predictions or decisions based on learned patterns and data. However, these models can encounter situations where they lack sufficient information, encounter ambiguous inputs, or extreme cases for which they were not specifically trained. This can lead to inaccurate or biased results. In-the-loop machine learning addresses these limitations by incorporating human feedback and intervention throughout the model lifecycle. This feedback can take various forms, such as data tagging, prediction verification, or corrective input. By involving human experts, the system can learn from their expertise and use their domain knowledge to solve complex or uncertain situations.

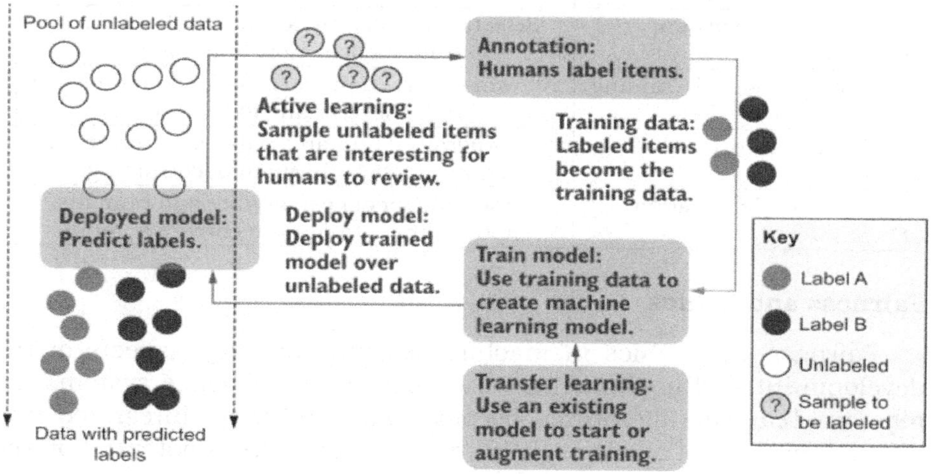

Human-in-the-Loop Machine Learning

The iterative nature of HIL ML allows for continuous improvement of the model over time. When the model makes predictions or decisions, people review and evaluate the results and provide feedback, which is used to refine and update the model. This feedback loop ensures that the system adapts and evolves, becoming more accurate, robust and reliable.

HIL ML has many applications in various fields. In healthcare, it can be used in the diagnosis of doctors by combining the knowledge of doctors with the analytical power of machine learning models. In autonomous vehicles, drivers can review and correct decisions made by the AI system to improve safety. In the context of content moderation, reviewer s can strengthen and refine decisions made by automated systems to reduce the risk of false positives or false negatives. However, implemen t ing HIL ML also brings challenges. This requires creating effectiv e communication channels between humans and machine learning systems, designing effective interfaces for human feedback, and addr e ssing issues of bias, privacy and ethics. Finding the right balance between human intervention and independent decision making is critical to system reliability and efficiency.

In general, human-loop machine learning is a collaborative approach that combines the strengths of humans and machines to create more accurate , robust and adaptive models. HIL ML strives to create AI systems t hat are reliable, transparent and compatible with human values by leveraging the power of human knowledge and control.

Technique	Description
Active Learning	Selectively querying labels from humans to train models more effectively.
Interactive Model Training	Allowing users to provide feedback and iterate on model training in real-time.
Human-Guided Labeling	Incorporating human feedback to correct or improve labels during model training.
Model Explanation	Presenting model explanations to humans, enabling them to provide corrective input.

Fairness and Ethics

Fairness and ethics in machine learning are key aspects of the developm e nt and implementation of artificial intelligence systems. As machine l earning algorithms become more and more integrated into different aspects of our lives, it is important to address potential biases and ethical issues that may arise.

Fairness in machine learning refers to the concept that people are treated fairly and without discrimination based on their protected characteristics, such as race, gender or age. Machine learning models can be inadvertently introduced through biased training data or faulty algorith m s, leading to discriminatory results. For example, if a facial recognit i on system is trained primarily on data from light-skinned individuals, it may struggle to accurately identify individuals with darker skin tones, thus maintaining racial segregation. To ensure fairness, it is necessary to develop unbiased algorithms, monitor training data, and continuously evaluate and monitor system performance to identify and correct potential anomalies.

Ethical aspects of machine learning include broader concerns about the effects and consequences of artificial intelligence systems on individuals and society. These aspects include data protection, transparency, accountability and the possibility that AI systems can be used for malicious purposes. Privacy concerns arise when machine learning algorithms process and analyze large amounts of personal data, raising questions about consent, data protection and potential misuse or unauthorized use. Transparency and explainability are important to ensure that people understand how AI systems make decisions, especially in areas such as healthcare or finance, where algorithmic decisions can have significant consequences. Accountability is important in situations where AI systems make mistakes or cause harm, ensuring mechanisms to correct the situation and hold those accountable.

In addition, ethical aspects are related to social effects, such as the possibility of artificial intelligence to exacerbate existing inequalities, automate jobs or influence public opinion by manipulating data. It is important to assess the potential consequences of AI systems before deployment, engage in cross-disciplinary discussions to assess the ethical implications and actively engage stakeholders in considering different perspectives.

Strategy	**Description**
Fair Feature Selection	Removing sensitive or biased features from the training data.
Bias Mitigation	Modifying models or data to reduce biased predictions.
Fairness Metrics	Defining and optimizing fairness metrics during model training.
Explainable Fairness	Combining fairness and interpretability to provide explanations for bias.

User-Centric Design

User-centered design for machine learning refers to an approach to the development and implementation of machine learning systems that focuses primarily on the needs, preferences, and experiences of end users. It recognizes that the ultimate goal of any machine learning application is to deliver value and solve real-world problems for users.

In user-centered design, the entire development process revolves around understanding the target users and their requirements. This includes conducting user research, gathering feedback and incorporating user insights into the design and development phases. By actively involving users from the beginning, machine learning models can be tailored to their specific needs, leading to more efficient and meaningful results. User-centered design emphasizes usability, simplicity, and intuitive user interfaces. It aims to create machine learning systems that are easy to understand, easy to use, and provide a seamless user experience. By considering factors such as user knowledge, accessibility, and contexts of use, designers can ensure that machine learning applications are not only accurate and effective, but also user-friendly and engaging.

In addition, user-centered design also considers ethical aspects and protects users' privacy. It recognizes the importance of transparency, explainability and trust in machine learning systems. Users must have a clear overview of the use of their data and be able to make informed choices about their participation. By prioritizing the ethical implications of machine learning algorithms, designers can create systems that adapt to user values and promote the responsible and fair use of technology.

In general, user-centered design for machine learning is a human-centered approach that prioritizes the needs and experiences of users. By understanding user requirements, designing intuitive user interfaces, and considering ethical implications, machine learning systems can deliver value, increase trust, and ultimately improve the overall user experience.

Consideration	Description
User-Friendly UI/UX	Designing intuitive interfaces that allow users to interact with the system.
Transparency	Providing clear information about how the system works and its limitations.
Customization	Allowing users to personalize the system according to their preferences.
User Feedback	Collecting user feedback to continuously improve the system's performance.

8.9. REAL-WORLD APPLICATIONS OF REINFORCEMENT LEARNING

Machine learning's reinforcement learning (RL) area is concerned with creating algorithms and models that can pick up information from their interactions with the environment in order to maximise a reward signal. In multiple fields, RL has found practical uses.

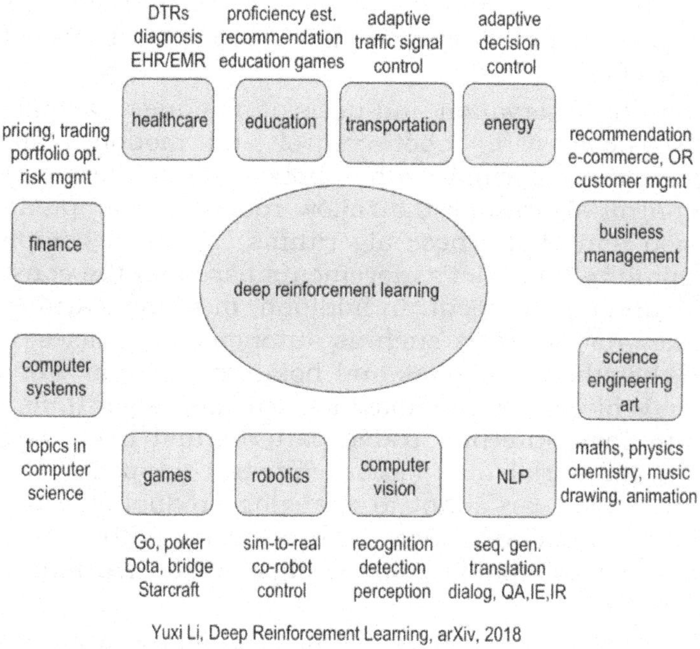

7 Real-World Applications of Reinforcement Learning

Robotics

Robotics in machine learning is an interdisciplinary field that combines the principles of robotics and machine learning to develop intelligent systems that can perceive and interact with the physical world. It involves integrating sensor technologies, actuators and control algorithms with machine learning algorithms to enable robots to acquire, process and analyze data from their environment and make informed decisions and actions based on that information.

One of the main goals of robotics in machine learning is to create autonomous robots that can learn from their experiences and adapt their behavior accordingly. Machine learning techniques such as reinforcement learning and deep learning are used to train robots to perform specific tasks by providing them with large amounts of data and allowing them to learn patterns and make predictions based on the data. This allows robots to learn new skills through trial and error and improve their performance over time. Robotic systems equipped with machine learning capabilities can perceive and understand the world using various sensors such as cameras, LIDAR, and tactile sensors.

They can process and interpret this sensory information using computer vision and pattern recognition algorithms, allowing them to recognize objects, navigate their environment, and interact effectively with people and other objects.

In addition to observation and decision making, machine learning robotics also deals with robot control and motion planning. By combining machine learning with robotics, researchers can develop advanced control algorithms that allow robots to manipulate objects with precision and skill. These algorithms can learn complex motor skills and optimize the robot's movements based on the constraints of a given task and environment. In addition, machine learning robotics will play a key role in areas such as autonomous vehicles, industrial automation, healthcare robotics and home automation. For example, autonomous vehicles rely on machine learning algorithms to sense their surroundings, interpret traffic patterns and make decisions in real time. In industrial automation, robots equipped with machine learning capabilities can adapt to changing production environments and optimize their performance. In healthcare, robotic systems can assist in surgery and rehabilitation, using machine learning to improve accuracy and safety.

Overall, robotics in machine learning represents a symbiotic relationship between two cutting-edge fields, enabling the development of intelligent robots that can perceive, learn and interact with the physical world. This interdisciplinary approach holds great promise to revolutionize various industries and create advanced robotic systems that can handle complex tasks and improve people's lives.

Autonomous Vehicles

Autonomous vehicles, also known as self-driving cars or driverless cars, are an important application of machine learning in the transportation industry. These vehicles use advanced machine learning algorithms and artificial intelligence systems to navigate and operate without human intervention. They can change the way we travel by improving road safety, making traffic more efficient and providing better accessibility.

Machine learning plays a crucial role in enabling autonomous vehicles to perceive and interpret their environment. These vehicles are equipped with various sensors, including cameras, lidar, radar and GPS, which collect vast amounts of information about the environment. Machine learning algorithms process this data to identify and classify objects such as other vehicles, pedestrians, traffic signs and road markings. By constantly analyzing and learning from this data, autonomous vehicles can make informed decisions and respond appropriately in real-time situations.

One of the main technologies used in autonomous vehicles is deep learning, a branch of machine learning that focuses on training multi-layered artificial neural networks. Deep neural networks can learn complex patterns and features from sensor data, allowing the vehicle to recognize and understand complex scenes. For example, they can detect objects, estimate their distance and speed, and predict their future movement. In addition, reinforcement learning algorithms are used to train autonomous vehicles to make optimal decisions based on specific objectives. Through trial and error, these algorithms learn to navigate different scenarios by receiving feedback in the form of rewards or punishments. By maximizing cumulative reward over time, an autonomous vehicle can adapt its behavior and learn effective strategies for tasks such as lane keeping, intersection control, and merging with traffic.

Another important aspect of autonomous vehicles is their ability to create and store high-resolution maps of their surroundings. Machine learning algorithms can process sensor data to create detailed maps that include information about lane restrictions, road signs and landmarks. These maps, combined with real-time sensor data, allow the vehicle to accurately locate itself on the road and plan safe and efficient routes.

However, developing fully autonomous vehicles that can operate in diverse and complex real-world conditions remains a major challenge. Ensuring safety and reliability are paramount as autonomous vehicles must make critical decisions in a dynamic and unpredictable environment. Machine learning algorithms need to be trained on huge amounts of diverse data, including rare and unusual scenarios, to improve their reliability and generalizability.

Game Playing

Gaming in machine learning means applying artificial intelligence techniques to develop intelligent systems capable of playing games. It is an exciting and challenging field that combines the principles of game theory, optimization and decision algorithms to create computer programs that can compete with human players or other artificial intelligence agents.

The goal of gaming in machine learning is not only to imitate human behavior, but to surpass it by designing strategies and algorithms that can make optimal decisions in a gaming environment. This means training AI models using large data sets of game examples, or using reinforcement learning methods, where the AI agent learns by interacting with the game environment and receiving feedback in the form of rewards or punishments.

Gaming in machine learning has received considerable attention due to notable achievements in games such as chess, go, and poker. IBM's Deep Blue, which defeated reigning world chess champion Garry Kasparov in 1997, and AlphaGo, which defeated world Go champion Lee Sedol in 2016, demonstrated the potential of artificial intelligence in mastering complex games.

One of the core challenges of gaming is the vast search space that must be explored to find the best move or strategy. To solve this, algorithms such as Monte Carlo Tree Search (MCTS) were developed, which simulate many game outcomes to estimate the value of each move. This allows AI agents to make informed decisions based on the probability of success.

In addition, machine learning gameplay outperforms traditional board games. This includes video games, online multiplayer games, and even real-time strategy games. AI agents can be trained to play against human opponents, cooperate with human players, or compete against each other, leading to advances in the development of intelligent gaming robots and virtual opponents.

Beyond the gaming realm, gaming in machine learning has a broader impact. The techniques and algorithms used in playing the game can also be used in other fields such as military strategy, logistics and resource allocation, where decision making under uncertainty and optimization is crucial.

Resource Management

Machine learning resource management refers to the efficient allocation and use of computing resources such as computing power, memory, storage, and network bandwidth to facilitate the training, inference, and deployment of machine learning models. As machine learning algorithms and models become increasingly complex and datasets grow, effective resource management becomes critical for optimal performance and scalability.

One aspect of resource management is hardware management. This includes selecting and configuring the appropriate hardware infrastructure for machine learning tasks. This includes the right combination of processors, graphics processing units (GPUs), memory capacity and storage devices to meet the computational requirements of the training and inference processes. Hardware management also takes into account factors such as scalability, cost-effectiveness and energy consumption.

Another important aspect is workload planning and optimization. Machine learning tasks often involve multiple steps, such as data processing, model training, hyperparameter tuning, and model estimation. Resource management systems must efficiently allocate resources between these phases, taking into account data dependencies, parallelism, and hardware limitations. Load balancing techniques, work scheduling algorithms and task prioritization strategies are used to ensure efficient use of resources and completion of various tasks in a reasonable amount of time. In addition, resource management includes memory management and data storage. Machine learning models often require large amounts of memory to store intermediate computations, training data, and model parameters. Efficient memory allocation, caching and garbage collection techniques can significantly improve performance and reduce memory overhead. Similarly, data storage solutions optimized for processing large data sets, such as distributed file systems or cloud-based storage services, play a crucial role in managing input and output data for machine learning tasks.

Additionally, resource management includes performance monitoring and tuning. Machine learning systems produce a significant number of performance metrics, including computational resource usage, model accuracy, training time, and inference latency. By monitoring these metrics, you can identify potential bottlenecks, optimize resource allocation, and make informed decisions about hardware upgrades or infrastructure changes. Technologies such as auto-scaling, adaptive resource allocation and dynamic workload balancing can be used to ensure effective and efficient real-time use of resources.

In general, machine learning resource management is a multifaceted discipline that focuses on optimizing the allocation and use of computational resources to support the training, inference and deployment of machine learning models. It covers aspects of hardware management, workload scheduling, memory management, data storage, and performance monitoring to achieve optimal performance, scalability, and cost-effectiveness in machine learning systems.

Finance

Finance and machine learning are two interrelated fields that have seen significant advances and applications in recent years. Machine learning, a subset of artificial intelligence, refers to the development of algorithms and models that allow computers to learn and make predictions or decisions without special programming. In the context of finance, machine learning techniques have been widely used to, among other things, analyze large and complex financial data sets, identify patterns and generate insights for investment decision support, risk management, fraud detection and portfolio optimization.

One of the most important advantages of machine learning in finance is its ability to process huge amounts of data and extract meaningful information from it. Financial markets generate vast amounts of data, including historical price and volume data, news articles, social media and financial indicators. Machine learning algorithms can process this data, learn from patterns and correlations, and create predictive models that can be used to predict future market movements or identify profitable business opportunities.

Machine learning algorithms are particularly useful in areas such as algorithmic trading, where speed, accuracy and the ability to process large amounts of data in real time are critical. These algorithms can analyze market conditions, historical prices and other relevant factors to automatically execute trades and optimize trading strategies. For example, high-frequency trading (HFT) firms rely heavily on machine learning algorithms to make split-second trading decisions and exploit short-term market inefficiencies.

Risk management is another area where machine learning has had a significant impact on finance. By analyzing historical data and identifying patterns, machine learning models can estimate the likelihood and impact of various risks, such as credit disruptions, market volatility or fraud. These models can help financial institutions improve their risk assessment processes, develop early warning systems and improve their ability to detect and prevent fraudulent transactions.

Portfolio optimization is another application of machine learning in finance. Machine learning algorithms can help investors create optimal portfolios that maximize return and minimize risk, taking into account a number of factors such as historical assets, risk appetite and market conditions. These algorithms can also continuously monitor the market and adjust a portfolio to changing conditions, enabling adaptive and dynamic portfolio management strategies. However, it is important to note that there are some challenges with using machine learning in the economy. Interpretation and explainability of machine learning models can be difficult, especially when dealing with black-box algorithms such as deep learning neural networks. In addition, there are concerns about potential bias in the data used to train these models, as well as the risks associated with purely algorithmic decision-making without human oversight.

Healthcare

Healthcare and machine learning have become a powerful combination that has revolutionized the way we approach diagnosis, treatment and patient care. Machine learning, a subset of artificial intelligence, refers to the ability of computer systems to analyze and interpret complex data patterns, learn from them, and make predictions or decisions. In healthcare, machine learning algorithms can be trained on vast amounts of medical data such as patient records, clinical notes, medical images and genomic data.

One of the most important applications of machine learning in healthcare is medical diagnosis. By leveraging large data sets, machine learning algorithms can identify subtle patterns in patient data that may not be obvious to human observers. This enables early and accurate detection of diseases such as cancer, cardiovascular disease and neurological disorders. Machine learning algorithms can also help predict risk, helping healthcare providers identify individuals at higher risk for certain diseases and enabling preventive interventions.

Another important area where machine learning is having a major impact is medical image analysis. Machine learning algorithms can help radiologists and pathologists detect abnormalities and provide more accurate and timely diagnoses by analyzing medical images such as X-rays, MRI scans and pathology slides. This can lead to faster treatment decisions, reduce human error and improve patient outcomes. Machine learning is also used to customize treatment plans and optimize drug therapy. Machine learning algorithms can help determine the most effective treatment options for specific patients by analyzing patient characteristics, genetic information, and treatment outcomes. The approach, known as precision medicine, tailors medical procedures to the unique characteristics of each patient, improving treatment effectiveness and reducing side effects.

In addition, machine learning plays a key role in healthcare operations and administrative tasks. It can help streamline hospital workflows, optimize resource allocation and forecast patient flow and demand. By analyzing historical data, machine learning algorithms can identify patterns that help hospitals and clinics improve operations and provide better patient experiences.

However, it is important to address the challenges of data quality, privacy and ethics in healthcare machine learning. Ensuring the accuracy and reliability of data used to train training algorithms, protecting patient privacy and maintaining transparency and fairness in decision-making are key aspects of implementing machine learning in healthcare.

Advertising and Marketing

Machine learning advertising and marketing has revolutionized the way companies communicate with their target audience and promote their products or services. Machine learning, a subset of artificial intelligence, uses complex algorithms and statistical models to analyze vast amounts of data and extract meaningful insights. In advertising and marketing, machine learning techniques are used to improve various aspects of campaigns, from audience targeting and segmentation to personalized messages and predictive analytics.

One of the most important benefits of machine learning in advertising and marketing is its ability to recognize and understand consumer behavior patterns. By analyzing historical data, machine learning algorithms can uncover hidden trends and preferences, allowing marketers to adjust their strategies accordingly. This data-driven approach allows companies to create highly targeted campaigns that respond to specific customer segments and increase the likelihood of engagement and conversion.

Machine learning also plays an important role in optimizing ad spend. By analyzing large data sets and real-time feedback, algorithms can make accurate predictions about the effectiveness of different ad placements, channels and ad variations. This allows marketers to allocate their budget more effectively and ensure that they are investing in the most promising means of reaching their target audience.

Personalization is another area where machine learning has had a significant impact on advertising and marketing. Using customer data such as demographics, browsing behavior and purchase history, machine learning algorithms can create personalized recommendations and messages. This level of personalization improves the user experience and increases the likelihood of conversion by presenting relevant content to consumers.

In addition, machine learning algorithms can analyze unstructured data such as social media posts, reviews and customer feedback to gain valuable insights. This sentiment analysis helps companies gauge public opinion about their products or services, identify areas for improvement, and respond quickly to customer concerns. By using machine learning, companies can proactively manage their brand image and build stronger relationships with customers.

Industrial Automation

Machine learning industrial automation refers to the integration of machine learning techniques and algorithms into industrial processes and systems to improve efficiency, productivity and decision making. This involves using advanced computing techniques to analyze vast amounts of data collected from sensors, machines and other industrial environments.

Using machine learning, industrial automation enables the development of intelligent systems that are capable of self-learning, adapting and making predictions based on data patterns and trends. This technology enables the automation of complex tasks that previously required human intervention, reducing human error and increasing overall work efficiency.

One of the main applications of industrial automation in machine learning is predictive maintenance. By constantly monitoring data from sensors embedded in industrial machinery, machine learning algorithms can identify patterns that indicate potential failures or malfunctions. This enables predictive maintenance, where maintenance procedures are planned before failure occurs, reducing unplanned downtime and optimizing resource utilization.

Another area where machine learning is advancing industrial automation is quality control and defect detection. Machine learning algorithms can analyze real-time data from cameras and sensors to detect defects or anomalies in products or manufacturing processes. This allows manufacturers to identify and fix problems in real time and ensure that only high-quality products reach the market. In addition, machine learning can be used to optimize industrial processes by analyzing large data sets and identifying relationships between input variables and process results. By modeling and predicting these relationships, machine learning algorithms can help optimize parameters such as temperature, pressure or flow rate, improving process efficiency and resource utilization.

In summary, machine learning industrial automation uses the power of data analytics and predictive modeling to transform traditional industrial processes. By automating tasks, predicting failures, ensuring quality and optimizing operations, it offers significant benefits in terms of efficiency, productivity and cost reduction in industrial environments. As technology advances, the integration of machine learning into industrial automation is likely to continue to innovate and improve industrial processes in the future.

Here is an overview table summarizing the real-world applications of RL:

Domain	Applications
Robotics	Grasping, manipulation, locomotion
Autonomous Vehicles	Self-driving cars, navigation

Domain	Applications
Game Playing	Go, chess, video games
Resource Management	Energy optimization, inventory management
Finance	Trading, portfolio management
Healthcare	Treatment recommendation, drug dosage
Advertising	Personalized ads, recommendation systems
Industrial Automation	Process control, energy optimization

8.10. MACHINE LEARNING'S FUTURE

Advancements in Machine Learning Algorithms

The development of machine learning algorithms has been at the forefront of research and development in recent years, leading to significant breakthroughs and transformative applications in various fields. Machine learning algorithms are at the heart of intelligent systems that can learn from data, identify patterns and make predictions or decisions without special programming.

One major advance is the rise of deep learning algorithms, particularly deep neural networks (DNNs). Deep learning has revolutionized the field by enabling the training of highly complex, multi-layered models capable of learning hierarchical representations from raw data. This has led to significant achievements in areas such as computer vision, natural language processing and speech recognition. Methods such as Convolutional Neural Networks (CNNs) have greatly improved image classification and object detection tasks, while Recurrent Neural Networks (RNNs) have been successful in sequential data analysis, including language translation and sentiment analysis.

Another area of progress is the development of reinforcement learning algorithms. Reinforcement learning focuses on training agents to interact with the environment, learning optimal actions through trial and error. The combination of deep learning and reinforcement learning led to impressive results, as evidenced by the AlphaGo program, which beat human champions at the game of Go. This combination has also proven successful in robotics, autonomous vehicles and resource management.

In addition, advances have been made in algorithms that address the challenges of limited labeled data, known as "fow-shot" or "zero-shot" learning. The purpose of these techniques is to enable generalization of patterns from a small number of examples, or even to learn new concepts without labeled examples. Approaches such as meta-learning, generative adversarial networks (GANs), and transfer learning have shown promising results in solving data scarcity problems.

In addition, researchers have explored algorithms that improve the interpretability and explainability of machine learning models. Because complex models such as deep neural networks often act as black boxes, understanding the reasons behind these decisions is critical, especially in sensitive industries such as healthcare and finance. Techniques such as alerting mechanisms, model distillation, and rule-based learning have been developed to provide insight into model predictions and provide transparency. Finally, efforts have been made to develop more efficient and scalable algorithms to meet the increasing demands of big data and real-time processing. Techniques such as stochastic gradient descent, mini-batch learning and distributed computing have made it possible to train models on massive datasets using parallel processing and cloud computing infrastructures. This greatly accelerated the training process and enabled the implementation of machine learning models in real-time sensitive applications.

Overall, advances in machine learning algorithms have pushed the industry forward, enabling significant advancements in various fields and paving the way for the widespread adoption of intelligent systems. The continuous innovation and improvement of these algorithms offers the potential for new breakthroughs and transformative applications in the future.

Increased Integration with Other Technologies

Machine learning as a field has made significant strides in recent years, and one notable trend is its greater integration with other technologies. This integration is driven by the need to use additional tools and techniques to improve the capabilities and effectiveness of machine learning systems.

One aspect of increased integration is the merging of machine learning and big data technologies. As the volume, velocity and variety of data increases, machine learning algorithms are combined with distributed computing frameworks such as Apache Hadoop and Apache Spark. These techniques enable massive data sets to be processed and analyzed in parallel, facilitating more accurate and scalable machine learning models. In addition, machine learning is closely intertwined with cloud computing. Cloud environments provide a scalable and flexible infrastructure for training and deploying machine learning models. Using cloud services, organizations can easily access powerful computing resources, manage large data sets, and deploy machine learning solutions globally. This integration also enables seamless collaboration and sharing of models and datasets across teams and organizations.

Another important integration is for edge computing. Edge devices such as sensors, wearables and IoT devices generate massive amounts of data that can be used for machine learning. By bringing machine learning models closer to the data source, processing at the device or edge can significantly reduce latency, improve privacy and minimize bandwidth requirements. This integration enables real-time, contextual decision making across industries including healthcare, autonomous vehicles and industrial automation.

In addition, machine learning is increasingly combined with natural language processing (NLP) and computer vision techniques. NLP allows machines to understand and process human language, enabling applications such as chatbots, sentiment analysis and language translation. Similarly, computer vision technologies enable machines to interpret and understand visual data, enabling applications such as object recognition, image classification, and autonomous navigation. By integrating these technologies, machine learning systems can understand the world more deeply and interact with people more intuitively and naturally.

Overall, greater integration of machine learning with other technologies will drive innovation and expand reach. This enables the development of more efficient and intelligent systems that can process large amounts of data, make informed decisions in real time and interact with people and the environment in more complex ways. As these integrations continue to develop, we can expect even more exciting advances in machine learning and its applications across industries.

Applications Across Industries

Machine learning has become an important part of various industries, changing the way companies operate and has had a significant impact on several sectors. Its applications span many fields, promoting innovation and efficiency. In the healthcare industry, machine learning is used in, for example, disease diagnosis, medical image analysis, drug development and personalized medicine. By analyzing large amounts of medical data, machine learning algorithms can help identify patterns and make accurate predictions, improving patient care and medical outcomes.

In the financial sector, machine learning has transformed processes such as fraud detection, credit assessment, algorithmic trading and risk assessment. Using machine learning algorithms, financial institutions can quickly detect fraud, assess creditworthiness, optimize business strategies and assess risks more accurately, improving operational efficiency and reducing financial losses.

Retail and e-commerce have also adopted machine learning techniques to improve customer experience, optimize inventory and enable targeted marketing campaigns. Recommender systems powered by machine learning algorithms analyze customer preferences and behavior, provide personalized product recommendations and increase customer engagement. In addition, machine learning algorithms enable retailers to forecast demand, optimize pricing strategies and automate inventory management, improving operational efficiency and profitability.

Machine learning plays a key role in the transportation and logistics industry as it optimizes route planning, demand forecasting and fleet management. By analyzing historical data and real-time data, machine learning algorithms can predict traffic patterns, optimize delivery routes and accurately estimate delivery times. It helps companies improve their operations, reduce costs and increase customer satisfaction.

In the energy sector, machine learning is used for predictive maintenance, energy consumption optimization and renewable energy forecasting. By analyzing sensor data and historical maintenance data, machine learning algorithms can predict equipment failures, enabling proactive maintenance and minimizing downtime. Machine learning also facilitates the optimization of energy consumption models, leading to better energy efficiency and savings. In addition, machine learning algorithms can predict renewable energy production based on weather conditions and historical data, helping to integrate and manage renewable energy sources.

In summary, machine learning has different applications in different industries. Machine learning is transforming processes, optimizing operations and driving innovation from healthcare to finance, from retail to transportation and energy to many others. Its ability to analyze vast amounts of data, identify patterns and make accurate predictions has made it a powerful tool for companies to make informed decisions, improve efficiency and deliver better products and services to customers.

Made in the USA
Monee, IL
04 November 2026

67381202R00115